HEBRIDEAN
MEMORIES

The author in 1964. Photograph by AW Robertson

HEBRIDEAN MEMORIES

SETON GORDON

FOREWORD BY ARTHUR W. FERGUSON

Neil Wilson Publishing

Neil Wilson Publishing Ltd
www.nwp.co.uk

© Seton Gordon Literary Estate, 2018
Foreword © Arthur W. Robertson, 1995

First published in 1923.
Second edition published in 1995.
Third edition published in 2011.
Reprinted 2012, 2018.

A catalogue record for this book is available from the British Library.

The author has asserted his moral right under the Copyright,
Designs and Patents Act, 1988, to be identified as Author of this Work

Print edition ISBN: 978-1-906476-21-2
Ebook ISBN: 978-1-906476-27-4

Designed by Melvin Creative
Printed and bound in the EU

CONTENTS

PART IV

Some Birds of the Hebrides

FOREWORD

THROUGH THE greater part of this century Seton Gordon observed and recorded the natural scene in the Highlands and Islands of Scotland; his many books already hold a special place in the literature of his native land. In his biography by Raymond Eagle, we learn that his mother Ella Mary Gordon wrote poetry which was esteemed by the Victorians and even the Queen herself. The poetess surely passed her literary gift to her son.

A naturalist by training and instinct, Seton Gordon's special interest was in birds, and the golden eagle always held a strong fascination for him. In the early days of bird photography he and his wife Audrey worked closely together to produce many superb pictures of a standard which even now cannot be bettered. Seton was an expert on alpine flowers and their distribution in Scotland. But he saw mankind also as part of the natural scene. Human ways of life which were linked with the land or sea he observed with sympathetic understanding. His deep knowledge of Highland history adds very much to the interest and value of his books.

All his life he was a great walker. A day for him was wasted if some, or preferably all of it, was not spent roaming under open skies, whatever the weather. In his unhurried travels he heard many a story about the bygone days of the clans, and fables of water monsters and fairies. Ancient and remote memorial cairns were visited. His writing gives us all this legendary or historic background, and the meaning and charm of Gaelic placenames are revealed. He loved the unique music of the highland bagpipe, the *Ceol Mor* or *piobaireachd*, which he played himself and used to judge at piping competitions. At all times he wore the kilt, except on rare and sad occasions when trousers were absolutely unavoidable! One of his favourite pipe tunes has the title *Sleam fhein an gleann* — 'The glen is mine'. It expresses the love he felt for all our heritage of glens and hills, and about which he wrote in words which flow as naturally as a Highland burn. Descriptions are often so vivid that we seem to be there with him ourselves.

Hebridean Memories, first published in 1923, is partly a picture of disappearing ways of life. There is a poignant account of an emigrant ship leaving for Canada. But the beauty of the islands dominates all — the magic is always there.

Arthur W. Ferguson

INTRODUCTION

THIS BOOK is an attempt to bring before the reader something of the peculiar attraction of the lonely group of Hebridean Islands which lie far to the west of the mainland of Scotland. Some of the chapters also tell of the charm of the Inner Hebrides and one or two treat of the Highlands of Argyllshire.

I have frequently heard mention that the West Highlander and Islander is a person of slow intelligence. It is true he lives far from civilization, and his intelligence is not so quick as that of the dweller of the town. But who of his critics takes into consideration the fact that English is a foreign tongue — a learnt language to him? For the speech of the dweller of the West Highlands and Islands is entirely Gaelic, and though he may converse in English tolerably well, and understand it too when spoken slowly and clearly, how can he be expected to talk it so fluently or intelligently as an Englishman or a Lowland Scot?

The Islesmen, and most of the West Highlanders as well, are bilingual, and that is more than many of their critics are. On the Islands, as elsewhere, varied types of people exist, but I think that nowhere in Scotland more charming personalities can be found. The best type of Islesman has a courtly dignity and is at ease in any surroundings. The hospitality of the Island people is unbounded — they delight in pressing upon the stranger the best that their house can provide, yet would not think of accepting payment for what they have given.

As I saw the emigrants from Barra, Benbecula, and South Uist embarking at Lochboisdale on the CPR liner *Marloch* one afternoon of last April, I could not but reflect how regrettable a thing it was that these fine Island people should be forced by circumstances to leave the well-beloved Islands of their birth for an unknown land, whence the older people among them will never return. 'Cha till iad gu brath.'

My readers will find some repetitions in the book; this cannot be avoided, as each chapter is complete in itself, and the book is not meant to be read as a consecutive narrative.

My thanks are due to the editor of *The Scotsman*, Chambers's *Journal* (The Fish of the Howmore) and other papers for permitting me to republish certain articles which originally appeared in these periodicals.

I hope this book will remind those of my readers who are familiar with the Hebridean coasts of the great fascination of the Western Isles and their wildlife;

those who do not know that country may, perhaps, be induced by this narrative to visit those wide and windy acres and understand the magnetism of the West, which induced the exile to write:

From the lone shieling of the misty island
Mountains divide us, and the waste of seas —
But still the blood is strong, the heart is Highland
And we in dreams behold the Hebrides.

SETON GORDON
Connel, Argyll.
June, 1923.

PART I
Spring Memories

CHAPTER I
A Sea-girt Home of the Peregrine

FROM THE extreme south-western shore of the lonely Hebridean isle of Tiree rises a storm-swept hill, Ceann a'Bharra. On its eastern side the hill is gently sloping, with grassy banks where hardy sheep graze and where, in April and May, many primroses and wild hyacinths bloom. Seaward, great cliffs descend sheer into the Atlantic, and on these dark, menacing rocks the peregrine falcon, the raven, and many kittiwakes, guillemots and green cormorants make their spring and summer home.

During the March of which I write few, very few, fine days cheered the western islands. Storm clouds almost constantly raced across the sodden land from the open spaces of the ocean, and the air was laden with salt spray and watery vapours.

But at length came a day when the sun shone brightly and the sky was clear, though a strong southerly wind swept across this island of little shelter.

During winter the lochs of the isle are peopled with many wild swans, from Iceland and the Siberian steppes. But today each loch was deserted, although upon that sheet of scarcely moving water known as the Faodhail fed three Bewick's swans — two parents with their only youngster of the previous season. A mile from them, where the stream has its source in an extensive bog, three whooper swans could lie seen. The two Bewick's swans were, I think, lingering here beyond their season for the sake of their young, for when they rose from the water to fly, with musical cries, backward and forward overhead, the immature swan did not accompany them, though in its direction they east many an anxious glance. The youngster had apparently received some recent Injury, tor its power of flight must have been unimpaired when, in autumn, it journeyed south from distant Siberia.

Above the 'machair', or level grazing land, lapwings rocked and swayed in impulsive flight, furiously pursuing any of the gull tribe that unwittingly trespassed overhead. Upon the short-cropped grass a flock of golden plover fed warily. In the clear air were many larks, each singing his hardest as he rose until he became a mere speck against a background of deep blue. From each ditch snipe rose, with curious scraping cry and arrow-swift swerving flight.

A nine-mile walk from the little village of Scarinish brought me to the slopes of Ceann a'Bharra, and for the first time for a week I was for a brief space in shelter from the wind. But although that spring had been boisterous beyond the average it had been mild, and already in mid-March the grass, even upon the hill slopes, was of that verdure which one associates with April and May. In the warm sunshine moths fluttered, and one sensed clearly the coming of the tide of full spring, and of the summer which would shortly follow.

As I commenced the short climb to the hilltop the wind veered round a little, and from the Atlantic swept a heavy, though short-lived, squall of hail and rain. In the warm sunshine which followed there was in the air the pleasant scent of growing grass and awakening life.

From a low, sandy shore half a mile to the westward came the deep booming sound of a heavy surf breaking without pause upon the white sands, and above the shore a cloud of salt spray hung. In summer the hill of Ceann a'Bharra, as I have said, is the home of many birds. Today only the outposts of these summer birds had arrived, but the peregrine throughout the year, has its home on these wild rocks. As I looked from the hilltop down upon the grim precipice with the troubled ocean beneath, the falcon darted from her inaccessible nesting ledge and, with harsh and oft-repeated cries, mounted into the air in the teeth of the breeze. It seemed curious that her anxiety should have been so acute, for the time of her nesting was as yet almost a month ahead. On at least three occasions she returned to the same ledge. Once, as she sailed swiftly across the cliff face, a great black-backed gull pursued her in determined manner, but the falcon heeded him not and easily outdistanced him.

Immediately beneath the ledge of the peregrine a green cormorant stood beside her half-completed nest. In the nest there lay a large, green pine branch, picked up, presumably, from the water's surface, for the nearest fir tree — on Tiree itself no tree of any kind can exist — was distant at least twenty-five miles from the cliff.

Few herring gulls had as yet arrived at their nesting ledges, but I was interested to see that numbers of kittiwakes — the latest of the gull tribe to nest — were floating buoyantly upon the sea near the cliffs and that some of them were already standing beside their old nests. The guillemots had not as yet come in from the open ocean, nor had the puffins arrived; but rock pigeons darted from their gloomy caves, and I was astonished to see a blackbird flit across the face of the cliff. This bird of sweet music was apparently a migrant, for no blackbird nests upon Tiree. Upon the hilltop a dead sheep lay; from it a raven rose, poised against the wind, and soared steadily high above the rocks.

There are but few hills, even in the romantic country of the Hebrides, with so wild and magnificently grand an outlook as Ceann a'Bharra. Here is the home of the tireless spirit of the Atlantic. Here are great caves, where the ocean swell thunders, and great rocks smoothed and polished by the constant action of wind and tide, and to the ear is ever present the deep boom of the surf.

Today, over the ocean, were spread many drifting showers, so that everywhere sun and rain strove for mastery, and blue skies and grey, misty squalls contended together. Southward, far into the Atlantic, rose the lonely lighthouse of Skerryvore, the home of almost constant storms. Midway between where I stood and the lighthouse, ponderous waves were breaking leisurely on that submerged rock known in Gaelic as *Bogha na Slighe*, or in English, the Rock of the Passage. It is a deadly obstacle for any ship out of her course in darkness or in thick weather.

About Skerryvore itself was a curious misty patch on the ocean. So bright was it that it seemed as though the sun shone here continuously, but the glass showed it to be caused by the surf from the great waves as they crashed, one after the other, upon the smooth-worn sides of the rock, their spume hanging in white fog around the lighthouse and causing the unusual effect. Here on Ceann a'Bharra I seemed to be midway between two distinct types of weather. From east to south the horizon was dark with heavy clouds of rain. The Isle of Mull was invisible, though nearer at hand the heavy swell might be seen leaping high against the dark, rocky sides of the small island known as Bac Beag, or the Little Dutchman.

From time to time, through drifting rain squalls, Iona showed; but away to the west, and especially towards the north-west, the sky was blue and the air clear. On Barra Head the sun shone brightly, and the lighthouse, although quite forty miles distant, was distinct. Then, bearing more northward, one could see other islands of the Outer Hebrides — Mingulay of the many cliffs, Barra with its conical hill, and even the lesser height of Easaval in South Uist.

Midway between Tiree and Barra the mailboat threaded her course. There is a fascination in watching the Atlantic waves as they play about rocks that are just showing above the tide. With each long wave the water, with slow and unhurried motion, engulfs the whole rock in a white flood of foam. No part escapes. And with the coming of the wave the air-filled waters show so many different colours — palest green, deepest blue, and all the shades of these colours, but each one perfect in itself. The wave passes. Down the steep sides of the rock there stream innumerable cascades of snow white water, contrasting sharply with the amethystine depths beneath them.

In its unhurried majestic speed, its tremendous strength, the Atlantic swell has its especial charm.

Above where the waves thundered rock doves darted to and fro, entering and leaving the gloomy caves where, in April, they would make their primitive nests. From the hilltop a curlew sprang with wild shriek of alarm.

Towards sunset the wind lessened. Over the sea there spread many lights of sun and shade, and the air had that clearness which foretells the near approach of rain. Upon the southern horizon lay a minute portion of a rainbow of brilliant colours — a 'wind dog' fishermen call such a phenomenon — and near it hung a hail squall, transformed by the unusual light to a thing of pale, sea-green colour as it descended to the ocean's surface.

At sunset the western sky burned with the last rays of the sun, shining through a narrow window from the gateway of *Tir nan Og*, or the mythical Land of Youth.

An hour later, with the coming of night, the new moon, with Venus close beside her, shone palely upon this Hebridean island, and in the quiet of the evening the cries of many lapwing, active by night as by day, carried far across the machair.

CHAPTER II
A Hill Loch and its Birds

IN THE hill country of the West, and set in a great expanse of wind-swept moorland, there lies a loch. No dwelling stands within sight of it, no road passes near. Indeed, so encircled is it by big hills, it has been seen by few. It lies high, and spring is late in setting her mark here. While in the strath below the larches are already green, and the birches are clad in most delicate and ethereal verdure, the banks of the loch are still brown and lifeless, for as yet the breath of spring has not penetrated thus far, to awaken the hill grass and the sweet gale that grows amongst it.

Although frost at times grips the loch, the water is more often, during the winter months, swept by terrific gales and lashing rainstorms from out the southwest, so that from the surface of the loch the spindrift is lifted and hurried forward in white whirling clouds upon the arms of the gale.

With the coming of April, if the season be kind, the sun shines warmly on the loch, and the heather and grasses on its banks are dried and heated. And during this fine weather one sees blue smoke rise from the surrounding moorlands, for the stalkers and shepherds are kindling the heather and hill grasses for the sweet young grass that this burning will later produce. The air, by afternoon, becomes hazy from the smoke of these many fires, and holds that distinctive and pleasant scent that is so often abroad upon the moorlands in April.

One morning in mid-April I made my way to the loch. The fine weather had left the hills for a while, and upon all the tops freshly fallen snow lay deep. From a treetop in the glen beneath, a missel-thrush sang loudly, and in a marshy field were many curlew and a pair of oystercatchers. On a ledge of rock at the burn side a pair of water ouzels had cunningly concealed their domed nest, built where the parent bird might noiselessly dive into the pool below at the approach of danger.

Amongst ancient, storm-scarred pines black game flew, and overhead a pair of kestrels hovered.

Out upon the open moorlands the wind, fresh from the south-west, was hurrying grey clouds past the hilltops. Across the corries swept at intervals heavy snow squalls.

It was noon when I reached the loch. The wind was backing, and the leaden sky betokened 'dirty' weather to come.

On the loch are many islands. On some there is no plant save heather, others give a roothold to sturdy birches — today still as leafless as in December.

Even the curlew do not come thus high except occasionally, but still the loch is the home of many birds.

On a rock far out in the loch and rising a few feet above the water were three cormorants. They had, I fear, lunched heavily upon trout, and were now digesting their meal, at peace with all the world. Near them swam a pair of beautiful black-throated divers.

On one of the larger islands a colony of herons were nesting. Upon their ungainly nests they sat clumsily, or else stood with evident pride over their new-hatched young.

Near them were lesser nests — those of the tribe of the grey crow. On a dead tree two cormorants had perched. A grey crow, flying up and also seeking a resting place, was driven off, but returned and perched precariously upon a slender branch out of reach of the cormorants.

As yet the sandpipers were not come to the loch, but the earliest and most hardy of summer migrants — the wheatear — was already here, and cheerily flitted among the boulders.

Away to the west the wind eddied about the great corries and, as its force increased, lifted the dry powdery snow and swept it far into the sky, where it stood out clearly against the leaden cumulus clouds.

Northward, a small moorland fire burned feebly. A drenching squall passed — and the fire had succumbed.

Evening was now drawing in, and with the dusk there came great banks of cloud, which enveloped all the hills. A drenching rain commenced to fall, hurried forward aslant the bitter wind. From the dripping heather a moorcock rose with vigorous crowing, and with his mate whirred his way across the dreary moor.

Through rifts in the cloud canopy the hills could be seen, already whitened afresh, and before nightfall each hill burn was a rushing torrent, thundering from the heights to the dark loch where, of a summer's evening, many trout rise and goosanders swim upon the placid surface.

A month later I paid a second visit to the hill loch.

A week of summer weather had come and gone, and for days the wind had blown fresh from the Atlantic, bringing with it many showers which fell as snow upon the hilltops.

By now the birches on the island where was the heronry were tinged with green, though not, as their neighbours of the glen below, in full leaf. The hill grasses, too, were commencing to grow, and amongst them — and already in flower — the petty whin (Genista anglica) and the lousewort (Pedicularis).

Swimming by himself was a widgeon drake, handsome in his full nesting plumage. His more sober-coloured mate was doubtless brooding her olive eggs upon some island on the loch. But an archenemy, or rather several of them, were near, for grey crows were nesting on the loch, and in more than one place I found the sucked eggs of grouse and ducks.

On one of the smaller islands, where wild anemones grew in profusion and the heather was long and of a great age, was a single heron's nest, built on the ground — an unusual situation for this bird — but with the eggs broken and apparently sucked.

Upon the birch-clad isle the herons had hatched their young, the infants shrieking huskily for food.

Beside the peat-stained margin of the loch, where great pine roots — relics of an earlier age — were exposed, sandpipers courted and a meadow pipit rose from her nest containing four eggs.

From a peat hag a greenshank rose with tuneful cry and sped forward on swift, clear-cut flight. Stags grazed near. They had shed their horns, and as yet the young antlers were not showing. A solitary curlew passed, with tremulous whistle, overhead, and out of the misty moorland came the harsh cry of a grey crow.

Not far from the loch is a small ruin. Few, I expect, who pass it know that here lived one of the most celebrated Gaelic bards. It is now centuries since he died, yet wherever the Gaelic language survives the songs of Duncan Ban McIntyre are still sung, for in them is a peculiar charm which appeals to all those who know and love *Tir nam Beann, nan Gleann, nan Gaisgeach* (The Land of the Hills and the Glens and the Heroes).

CHAPTER III
A Hebridean Pass in Spring

THE SEASON of springtide has always an especial charm, and nowhere is it more welcome than in the land of the Hebrides. Here winter is always severe. There may be, it is true, little frost and snow, but instead fierce storms from the Atlantic rush across the islands without a break for weeks on end. Rain-laden winds shake the crofters' houses, lift boats bodily into the air as though they were made of matchwood, and snatch up in spindrift the waters of the sea.

Mull is an isle of contrasts. Its western lands are altogether storm-swept — Treshnish, Loch nan Ceall, the Ross or promontory that leads down from Loch Buie to Iona. Yet in the centre of the island are great hills and grassy corries where, no matter from what quarter the wind may blow, there is always shelter for sheep and deer, and where the winter's snow may linger until mid-July in north-facing corries where the sun cannot reach it. Through the heart of these hills leads an ancient track, deserted now save for an occasional shepherd or a crofter from the Ross making his long journey to the port at Salen on foot, but formerly much used both in summer and winter.

Alongside Loch Ba the track winds, then traverses a deep glen — Glen Clachaig. Near the head of the glen it crosses a stony hill face, where it is known as Mam Clachaig, then drops again and reaches sea level near the head of Loch Scridain.

Early on a quiet April morning one hears in the birch woods which lie about the head of Loch Ba the low, bubbling notes of many blackcocks, assembled to fight, as their custom is each morning, from dawn until sunrise. From the glen beyond the woods come the tremulous whistling calls of curlew, which echo between the steeply rising hills, filling the still air with mournful sound in which is expressed the spirit of the moorland and of the wild places.

In this country the eagle formerly nested, but for the past half-dozen years the eyrie has been tenantless. Can it be that the eagles had reached so great an age that they were no longer able to rear a brood? It would seem so, for the birds were never far from their glen and the big hills which surround it until a twelve-month ago. Then one of the pair met with some mishap — a keeper's trap, maybe, set for lesser game, or a 'sportsman's gun' — and the survivor now sails alone above the hilltops.

But this April day, as I passed up the glen, there came, circling over me at a great height, three golden eagles, and one of them appeared to be doing his best

to drive off the remaining pair. It seemed as though the ancient chief were assert-
ing his rights against the newcomers — from Morvern, it may be, or from
Ardnamurchan — for the feathers were flying and the attack was still in progress
when the three birds, rising high above the summit of Beinn Mor, appeared as
black specks against a white, fleecy cloud drifting across the great expanse of blue.

One hoped that the newcomers might gain possession of the glen, for in Mull
the eagle is on the verge of extinction.

Not far from Mam Clachaig is a sunbathed corrie.

So steeply to the south does it lean that the little burn which drains it falls to
the sea loch far below in a series of cascades, with pale green pools of a wonderful clearness between them. Here was shelter from the keen east wind, and upon
the grassy slopes the sun shone with great power.

One remarked on the absence of snow from the high ground. Even the great
hills of the mainland far to the eastward were almost snow-free; only upon the
summit of Ben Nevis was the snowy covering continuous.

From the Ross of Mull rose the blue smoke of many heather fires, drifted quickly westward by the freshening breeze and creeping low over the ground as smoke
does in a strong wind.

South-westward, beyond the Ross, the sun sparkled on the waters of the open
Atlantic, where the small and lonely rock of Dubh Hirteach shows faintly against
a waste of seas.

On either side of the small corrie where I stood, big rocks rise. From the cliffs
to the westward came harsh and confused sounds and a raven appeared, with a
pair of grey crows in close pursuit. The raven had apparently trespassed on the
beat of the crows, and was being driven off angrily.

Above the larger cliffs on the east side of the corrie the raven paused, then circled slowly round, frequently closing its wings and shooting almost vertically
earthward.

Doubtless to mislead me, the dark bird now flew back across the corrie, circling
awhile above a herd of grazing hinds, which moved off uneasily at its appearance.
But the cunning of the raven at its nesting grounds is proverbial, and I felt sure
the nest was near. It was not long before a careful 'spy' across the corrie revealed
the nest — placed near the top of that rock above which the parent bird had
paused. The bleached heather stems of which it was made glistened in the bright
sunlight, and the white droppings from the almost-fledged young birds rendered
it the more conspicuous.

Although most keepers class raven and grey crow together as 'vermin', there is
amongst the shepherds and sheep farmers of the West a pleasing tolerance of the
raven. On all sides it seems to be agreed that it is not nearly so destructive to
lambs or game as the grey crow.

As I passed beneath their nest both ravens flew anxiously around, with oft-repeated croak, but keeping well out of gunshot.

'Thou hast raven's knowledge' is a saying amongst the Gaels, for the Clan MacDougall bird is credited with wisdom beyond all the birds of the air. Even in earliest times the raven entered much into the life of the western people. It is the mascot bird of the Clan MacDougall, and was taken by their chiefs of early days on all voyages of discovery. On one of these expeditions the first raven was liberated after the galley had been at sea for a number of days. The isles men were steering north, and, knowing the unerring instinct of the raven for the nearest land, hoped that the released bird would fly before them, showing that an undiscovered country lay ahead. But, to their disappointment the bird made its way back in the direction whence they had come. The next day a second raven was loosed. For a time it circled overhead, then returned to the boat. From its behaviour it was surmised by the intrepid explorers that they were far from any land, but during another day and night they kept on their northward course and then the third raven was liberated. Without hesitation it flew forward in the direction in which they were sailing and, following the course taken by the bird, an unknown land — Iceland — was shortly afterwards sighted.

The banner of the Clan MacDougall had woven upon it the form of a raven. Before a fight, if the banner fluttered bravely, so that the raven appeared to fly, it was held to be a favourable omen. The raven was also the emblem on the sacred standard of the great Odin. In the sagas, it is stated that Odin owned two ravens which, his inseparable companions, traversed great distances, and on their return to their master whispered in his ear the information they had gained during their travels.

The raven is the earliest bird to nest, and recently it was thought that the reason for this unusually early nesting had been discovered. This was that the raven brood was fed upon the placenta of the sheep — the tissue which passes the nourishment from parent to offspring and which is shed immediately after the birth of the lamb.

This theory does not, however, hold good in all districts. In the Isle of Mull I examined, during the early days of a recent April, four ravens' nests, all containing well-grown young, and one with feathered brood almost ready for flight. Now this was ten days before the commencement of the lambing season, which, in Mull, does not begin much before the 19th of the month. But even although the young raven broods may at times be fed on the placental membrane of sheep, it must not be imagined that the sheep suffer injury — they may not even be near at the time — though doubtless a shepherd seeing a raven beside his flock during the critical season of lambing might well draw such a conclusion. I am fully prepared to admit that the sable bird may sometimes mutilate a sickly ewe or a feeble lamb, but the harm done is very slight.

In the small glen that leads from the corrie of which I write is a stunted and storm-scarred oak. It grows at the foot of a waterfall and during a flood, when the burn thunders through the glen in a white, foaming torrent, its veteran branches are bathed in spray. A small and insignificant tree is this, yet by all the heron tribe of the district it is used as a nesting place.

The sun was low in the west as I reached the tree. The herons were without suspicion, for I had stalked them carefully, and from a distance of only a few feet they could be seen sitting — or 'lying', as the West Highlander more accurately describes it — on their nests. On a sunny bank one of their number, free from family cares, dozed peacefully, prostrate on the ground. As I watched the strange scene a heron, returning from his fishing in the sea loch beneath, flew up the glen homeward. His horror upon seeing a human intruder so close to his clan — and unperceived, too — was expressed in a succession of rasping cries, harsh and altogether unmusical. Their effect on the colony was electrical. With one accord the birds sprang upright, fully alarmed, yet uncertain from which quarter danger threatened. But as the shrieked-out warnings from the bird overhead were renewed the colony rose in a body, leaving unguarded seven nests, just below the level of the top of the waterfall, and only a few feet from me. In all the nests, save two, there lay unspotted eggs of a very beautiful sky-blue colour. In these two nests small youngsters with heads covered with long, hair-like bristles, were wheezing hoarsely and reproachfully at being so rudely disturbed.

Upon the sea loch far beneath, the floodtide forced its way against the breeze. In the last pool of the burn red-breasted mergansers fished, while amongst the budding bog myrtle nearby stonechats flitted cheerily as a perfect day of spring drew towards its close.

CHAPTER IV
A Western Corrie and its Wildlife

THE SUN rose upon a world whitened with frosty rime one April morning. The sky was cloudless, and of that deep, clear blue which betokens the best of weather.

At daybreak the hills of the Isle of Mull were hidden in soft, floating mists, but with the coming of the sun these were slowly dispelled. At first the snow-encrusted hilltops alone were visible, rising above the mist-sea; but by nine o'clock the whole island lay in brilliant sunlight, with Beinn Mor, greatest of its hills, glistening in its snowy coat.

Such weather in April is rare in the humid west, but ever since the first week in March the western seaboard and Hebrides that season had been favoured with weather more brilliant than the eastern districts could have imagined, with their leaden skies, constant snows and bitter North-easters.

Buried deep among the western hills is the corrie of which I write. From only one point can it be seen, and that the north. At the foot of the corrie a lochan lies. Here bright plumaged goosanders swim of a spring morning, and perhaps a mallard or two and a flight of widgeon.

It was from the shore of the lochan that my wife and I commenced our climb into the corrie at midday.

The morning frost had gone; on the steep hillside the sun shone warmly, so that lizards were enticed from their winter lairs and more than one tortoiseshell butterfly flitted aimlessly by on its fragile wings.

The moisture from the frost still lay upon the hill grasses and the heather, so that as yet no moorland fires dimmed the blue of the sky. A steep climb of a thousand feet, a narrow ridge to be crossed, and then one looks down into the corrie.

On the ridge hinds were feeding; from the lower grounds rose the trilling cries of courting curlew. Upon the drier ground the smallest and most prostrate of our stag mosses — *Lycopodium alpinum* — grew plentifully, but as yet no sign of life showed amongst any of the hill plants that existed upon this wind-swept ridge.

A keen breeze from the north brought at this height (2000ft above the sea) winter on its breath, though out of the wind the sun was delightfully warm.

One remarked upon the exceptional amount of snow carried by all the higher hills. Most of it fell at the New Year, and during the past month was frozen each night, and each day slightly thawed by sun heat, so that now its surface was as hard as iron and treacherously slippery.

They are very conical, these western hills, as compared with the more lofty Cairngorm summits. Beinn Chalium, Beinn Mor (above Crianlarich), Beinn Oss, Beinn Laoigh, all have tapering summits, with narrow and windswept ledges leading up to them, now thickly plastered with snow.

Of these hills which lie about the county march between Argyll and Perth, the most gently sloping is Beinn Dubhchraig, and it, this April day, resembled an ice-capped hill of Spitsbergen, so enveloped was it in snow to a depth of many feet — and even yards. Not a single black speck showed over all its wide northern face, into which furious winter storms from the south had drifted the whirling, powdery snows.

From lesser, snow-free hills blue smoke was now rising. One column of smoke ascended straight into the windless air. Another fire, on a more exposed hillside, was spreading rapidly before a fresh breeze.

From the ridge one looked full into the corrie. It lay, calm and restful, in the strong sunshine, and perhaps four hundred feet beneath. Past peat hags, where stags love to roll during the season of their autumn restlessness, the way led. At first the slope was gentle and grassy, but soon became steep, with an icy field of winter's snow covering it. Across the snow the tracks of deer showed. They had been made when the snow was soft; today the surface was so frost-bound that one's feet made no impression upon it.

Beyond the corrie and the glen beneath it there rose a multitude of snowy peaks.

The hills of the Black Mount forest — Stob Choire an Albannaich, Stob Gabhar and Clachlet — were of unrelieved white. Beyond them rose the rocky slopes of Bidean nam Beann and the lofty level summit of Ben Nevis. On the north-eastern horizon the sky was overcast, and one suspected that the fine weather of the West did not extend across Scotland.

In the corrie a heather fire burned. He who lighted it must have returned to his home in the glen below — for the corrie was deserted — leaving the fire to burn itself out at the margin of the snowfields near the head of the corrie.

An amphitheatre of rocks half-encircled the corrie, and from the rocks there hung enormous icicles. Where in less Arctic weather a burn drops in a thin cascade over the cliffs, these icicles were quite fifty feet in height, and of extra ordinary beauty. All the more striking did they appear on account of the black rocks immediately behind them.

On an ice-encrusted ledge were the flattened remains of an eagle's eyrie. One looked carefully through the glass to see whether the eyrie showed any trace of recent occupation. At that very moment there appeared in the deep blue sky a small black speck. At a great speed this object rushed earthward, showing itself, as it neared the corrie, to be nothing less than a golden eagle. Straight down upon the far cliff the eagle swooped, and as she alighted near the foot of the rock the glass revealed her new eyrie, not more than a couple of yards from her. Standing for a moment to scan the corrie, and evidently unaware of the proximity of the human species, the eagle walked up to her nest and settled herself upon it.

As one watched her there the warmth on the sunny side of the corrie was as of a summer's day. Blaeberry plants were opening their buds; in the peat stood ancient pine stumps, half buried.

It was, perhaps, thirty minutes later that the sun's heat dislodged one of the great icicles that hung from the rock above the eagle's nest. It fell with a splinter-ing crash, and the alarmed eagle spread her broad wings and sailed out over the corrie, disappearing across the hilltop beyond.

The eyrie was built upon a wide ledge of rock, some ten feet up from the foot of the cliff. It was not difficult to reach from below, and one could not but won-der why the birds had chosen so accessible a spot for their nest.

The eyrie was built chiefly of birch sticks. They had been broken from the liv-ing tree, for upon them green buds showed.

A piece of sheep's wool had been built into the nest, and two sprigs of heather. The two eggs lay upon a carpet of *Luzula sylvatica*, a grass-like plant invariably chosen by the golden eagle for the lining of her eyrie. One of the large, rounded eggs was richly spotted with brown, the other was white and unmarked.

Beside the ledge of rock delicate pink buds of the rose root (*Sedum rhodiola*) were showing, and from a minute quantity of soil adhering to the face of the rock grew a plant of *Saxifraga oppositifolia*, already in all the beauty of its bloom.

In contrast to the almost lifeless hillside and the icicles which hung above it, the small crimson blossoms of this purple mountain saxifrage were a delight to the eye. A very different place was this western corrie to that barren island off Spitsbergen — Hermansen Island by name — where I had last seen this saxifrage in blossom in mid-July. Upon this Arctic isle almost the only plant to maintain a root-hold is this small, prostrate saxifrage, and the blossoms on the countless thousands of its plants tinged the bleak isle with all the glory of a Scottish hill-side in August. It is in Scotland, as in Spitsbergen, the very first plant to flower upon the melting of the snows; but the season of its blossoming is a very short one.

Not far from the eagle's nest a tiny brown wren flitted, mouse-like, about the banks of a small burn. Rare is the corrie without its 'Jenny wren', however bleak and windswept it may be. There is a Gaelic tradition that the birds, once upon a time, decided to elect a king. That honour, they agreed, should be held by the bird which should fly highest.

All thought that the eagle must be successful, but when that proud bird had reached a great height a little wren, which had concealed itself upon the eagle's back, now emerged and mounted above the eagle, which was so dismayed at the audacity of its small adversary that it did not attempt to climb above it. To the wren, therefore, the proud title of King of Birds was accordingly given.

At sunset many stags made their way to the foot of the corrie. A few had shed their antlers, but the majority still retained their winter horns, one beast with a fine wide head and another with thirteen points attracting attention.

With the setting of the sun the air became intensely cold. Upon the shallow pools a thin layer of ice quickly formed, and the snow-laden hills stood out coldly against the darkening sky. From a young plantation came the bubbling of blackcock, and in the gathering dusk a woodcock flew overhead with curious erratic flight and sibilant cry.

CHAPTER V
A May Snowfall in the Hebrides

MAY IS ever an uncertain month and more often than not she brings to the hills and moorlands a fleeting snowstorm. The 'teuchats' storm' it is sometimes named in the east of Scotland, for it numbs the clan of the green plover as they brood their far-incubated eggs; it may even drive the plover and curlew to the low-lying glens. But to the West these storms of late springtide rarely come, so that the May snowstorm that visited the Inner Hebrides in the spring of which I write – 1921 – was the most severe for many years. How extreme were the contrasts in weather that spring! Two days before the snow midsummer reigned over all the western seaboard. For a full week the sun had shone steadily. Scarce a puff of wind stirred the Atlantic. Even the long swell was stilled, for the fine weather extended far out to sea. Toward afternoon the air each day was thick and hazy from the smoke of many moorland fires, for the season of heather burning had been extended that year until the last day of April. Even during the opening days of May one still saw isolated fires, although, with the young grass already commencing to grow, such late burning is apt to do more harm than good.

The snow came unexpectedly to the West; on the last day of the fine weather that preceded it I crossed a wild and rocky isle, now given over to the raven, the buzzard, and the hill sheep. On a rock just above the silent waters no fewer than twenty-seven seals basked, scratching themselves leisurely and quaintly with their flippers and enjoying to the full the warm sunshine.

Amongst them was a single grey seal, distinguished from the rest by his larger size and silvery-grey dappled coat.

Swimming on the unruffled water beyond, a great northern diver displayed his handsome nesting plumage as he paused awhile on passage to his Arctic nesting grounds, perhaps on some hill-tarn of Iceland. He had captured a flounder, and struggled desperately to swallow his prize, so that the waters around him became troubled and many ripples spread over the glassy surface. From a rocky ledge a buzzard soared out lazily; near the spot his mate left her nest, placed where it could be reached with little difficulty. In the nest were three eggs, two richly marked, the third unspotted and bluish in colour. A fresh-pulled branch of larch lay in the nest. From its soft, green needles the sun was drawing a delicious scent. Near it was laid a green frond of fern. The buzzard and eagle both decorate their nests with green branches, even when their young are almost full-grown. Can it be that they have developed in them the aesthetic sense? A pair of ravens were nesting near the buzzards, their young already well-grown and gasping in the windless air. Raven and buzzard do frequently nest beside each other, possibly for mutual protection, for there is no liking lost between them.

Far up the hill seven wild goats fed, and above them wandering buzzards soared.

Near the western end of the island the cliffs are high, and here I came across another pair of nesting buzzards with their attendant pair of ravens. As the two different birds approached each other, the ravens attacked their large enemies fiercely, the latter, when hard-pressed, turning on their backs and striking up viciously with their talons.

The ravens upon this island are left by the owner undisturbed, and it was curious to see how different was their behaviour to that of members of their race living within reach of the vermin-killing keeper. The hen bird — for by her behaviour I took her to be the female — showed keen anxiety, flying round me with oft-repeated croak and at times alighting on a ledge near the top of the cliff, where she uttered curious cries as of cork-drawing. When persecuted the raven shows great cunning, and even when the young are in danger does not approach the nest.

As I lay with my long glass on the hillside a stoat hurried past me, eagerly searching for some victim. To my surprise a rabbit, appearing from its burrow, chased away the marauder in a fury, pursuing it for a considerable distance and then leisurely returning, full of its own importance.

That night the cuckoo sang from the leafy plantations, swallows hawked flies, and midges were abroad in numbers, unwelcome and persistent in their attack. It was as though midsummer were come and in her most gracious mood.

But early next morning a chill wind from the north swept the Hebrides. All day it continued, parching the primroses and wild hyacinths where they peeped with glorious blue flower-heads from amongst the quickly springing bracken. Through the night there came a blizzard of snow. At daybreak the flakes were of unusual size, and fell incessantly hour after hour. At midday the fall slackened, the clouds lifted, and the deep blue of the sky was revealed. Summer had indeed gone, and in her place full winter reigned supreme.

To the edge of the tide the ground was snow-clad, and the sea was of a cold, steel-blue colour. Across the slopes of Beinn Mor, dazzlingly bright in the sunlight, the snow was being drifted in clouds. That afternoon I crossed a 'bealach' or hill pass. At 1000ft above the sea an average depth of eight inches of snow covered the ground, and drifts several feet in depth hid each burn and sheltered hollow. Through these snowy wastes the hill sheep floundered helplessly; even the deer found progress difficult. The strong May sunshine had little effect upon the snow, so keen was the north-easter, and the drift at sunset still eddied about the hilltops, although at the shore the ground showed black at nightfall.

Golden plover, driven from their nesting grounds, haunted the grassy fields, and curlew were with them. A few days before I had heard the first whimbrel — most regular of birds in its coming — but during the storm the 'May bird' was not to be seen. It would be interesting to know what the bird world must think of such an untimely storm. It must be to them doubly bewildering, arriving so closely after a midsummer spell. In their nests the young herons — some of them already fledged — shivered in the bitter cold. Far up among the hills, in a deep and narrow gorge into which the snow had drifted, the brood of a pair of ravens crouched low. But the raven is a hardy bird, and scarcely a year passes without the young being exposed to frost and snow.

A luckless sheep had fallen to the foot of the ravine and was imprisoned there. It still lived, and had eaten every living thing within its reach. With difficulty the precipitous face was descended, and with still greater difficulty — and after many unsuccessful attempts — the struggling animal was carried to the hillside above.

Towards evening, after a heavy snow shower, frost gripped hill and glen. The birds were silent. No thrush or blackbird sang; not even the ring ouzel fluted from the solitary rowan far up the hillside. But the shore of the Atlantic is never altogether silent, and here oystercatchers piped at the edge of the tide, and mergansers in their courting swam and dived with incredible speed.

CHAPTER VI
The Whooper Swan

FEW PEOPLE are able to distinguish the whooper swan from the semi-domesti-cated mute swan, which, in its true wild state, inhabits Poland, Rumania and Denmark. The difficulty of distinguishing between the two species is increased by the fact that the mute swan inhabits some of our lochs in an almost wild state; indeed, it is not certain that it may not visit the British Isles from its Continental haunts from time to time. But, although they may be superficially alike, there are several points of marked difference between the two species. In the first place the neck of the mute swan is held in a curve; the whooper's neck is often carried straight and goose-like. Then there is a striking difference in the bill. That of the mute swan is reddish-brown in colour, and at the base is a pronounced knob or 'berry'. The whooper's bill lacks this 'berry', and in colour is black at the tip and bright orange-yellow towards the base. The 'whooping', deep-toned call note of the whooper is characteristic, while the mute swan, as its name implies, is silent, or almost so.

Up to the end of the eighteenth century the whooper swan nested in Orkney, but more recently it was imagined to have become extinct as a breeding species in the British Isles, and it was believed that its nearest nesting ground was Iceland. It is interesting, therefore, to be able to record that at least two pairs, and probably several more, have nested for the past few seasons in the Western Highlands. *

It was on a rough and cold April day that I first saw the whoopers at their nest-ing loch. On the hills snow was drifting, and there was nothing to suggest the arrival of spring. But a month later — the date was May 21st — when my wife and I again visited the loch of the swans, the young grass was beginning to push through the dense masses of dead vegetation, and the few birches that grew beside the loch were clad in filmy green. The day was wild and stormy. Mist drove across the hills; rain and wind lashed the waters of the loch. It was almost by chance that we found the whooper's nest. Passing a large island, where a colony of herons were nesting, a swan swam out ahead of us.

* *For two consecutive years to my knowledge a pair of whoopers have hatched their young successfully on this loch. During the present season (1923) for the first time two pairs of these wild swans nested on the islands. One nest is still intact as I write, the other has been robbed by collectors.*

By her behaviour she gave no indication that she was brooding, yet we came upon the nest, containing four dirty white eggs, almost at once. The nest was about five yards from the water's edge. It had apparently been used for several years in succession, judging by its weather-beaten appearance, and was built of dead grass and moss piled high. Beside it were the remains of an earlier nest. A well-marked track led from the nest to the shore; evidently it was the habit of the swan, after landing an a small gravelly beach, to dry her feathers on a little knoll of green grass before walking to her eggs, for on this knoll many of her feathers were lying. The ground favoured the construction of a rough hiding-place. The walls of the observation post were made of turf, cut with a spade from the soft ground above the water's edge, and the roof was formed by a piece of canvas, supported on sticks, and then likewise covered with sods of blaeberry plants. It was a very good 'hide' and was almost invisible, so well did it harmonise with its surroundings.

The following morning brought with it a complete change of weather. The sky was blue, a gentle northerly breeze stirred the waters of the loch. Each hill stood out, and in the clear light each lingering snowfield was dazzling white. A belated swallow moved past on its migration; greenshank fluted in the peat bogs. In a bay a pair of black-throated divers were fishing. As we rowed towards the island we saw the swan sail out on to the blue waters and join her mate feeding near the opposite shore.

It is useless to enter any hiding-tent unless one is accompanied by a companion, and unless that companion departs as ostentatiously as possible. All birds can count one, but very few more than one: so a human figure obviously leaving their nest stills their suspicions and causes them to return without delay, provided they have become accustomed to the presence of the hiding-tent, which should, if possible, be erected a few days previously.

At five minutes after midday I was shut into the hide by my wife, who subsequently rowed away from the island. In about twenty minutes one of the swans — I presumed the female — flew right overhead, calling loudly. A little later on she appeared, stood a moment or two near the water's edge, then, becoming suspicious, vanished from my view (which was somewhat restricted). She soon returned, however, and her fears being allayed, landed on the little beach and walked to the grassy knoll. Here she stood awhile, wiping and drying her breast feathers carefully by rubbing them with her head. This task finished to her satisfaction, she walked up to her eggs and settled down comfortably on them.

A meadow pipit chirped cheerfully from the long heather; herons grunted harshly, a chaffinch in a birch tree nearby repeated his tuneful little song.

My hiding-place was about fifteen feet from the swan's nest. I had feared she might notice and suspect the large lens of the camera fixed upon her; but if she did see it, she was indifferent. At first she seemed suspicious, and sat alert, with her long neck erect. But gradually she gained confidence, and commenced to work at the edges of her nest and its lining. Then, with a great deal of effort, she turned over one of the eggs with her bill. The male bird stood all this time near to the nest, perched on a stone rising from the water's surface, but he never once landed on the island.

The strong sun beat fiercely down. The whooper swan gradually became drowsy, and at length buried her head beneath her wing, her neck lying along her back in tortuous curves, and fell fast asleep. She was awakened by the grating of the returning boat as it was beached on the far side of the island. The swan instantly shot up her long neck, and a moment later ran hurriedly to the water's edge, swimming rapidly away.

The next morning we again visited the swans. After a night of white frost the morning was even finer and warmer than the preceding one. The sky was of a deeper blue, and there was a delightful feeling of young summer in the air. On the path to the loch lay a hen grouse freshly killed — perhaps the work of a fox — and her mate rose 'becking' a few yards away.

At 11.30am I entered the hide. The swan soon returned, and I took a number of photographs. Before she left the eggs to feed, about an hour later, she covered them carefully with pieces of dry grass. On her return, instead of removing this covering, she at once settled down on the eggs, and with her breast feathers pushed aside, or pressed down, the layer of grasses.

It was a most interesting experience to watch this swan at such close quarters. During the winter months one frequently sees whooper swans, on migration from Iceland, perhaps, upon the lochs of Scotland, but these travellers are usually wary and do not permit of a near approach.

That afternoon thunderclouds appeared above the hilltops, the sun was obscured, and in the air was a strange stillness as we left the hill-girt loch of the wild swans.

It was mid-December when again we passed near the loch. A full gale from the west was lifting the waters in spindrift. Yet the air was mild, and even on the highest tops there was but a slight powdering of snow.

The swans had now been joined by others of their tribe from overseas and with their full-grown young brood rode the waves buoyantly. Toward afternoon, although the gale continued unabated, from time to time a watery sun showed himself. As the wind veered the temperature quickly fell, and stinging showers of hail and sleet swept the moor, so that a wandering raven scarce made progress against the storm. From Ben Nevis the young snow was caught up on the arms of the gale and whirled in the form of driving mist far over the hilltop. And yet, so light a covering of snow had fallen, the hill was scarce grey with it.

Far to the west the waters of the Atlantic were lashed by the storm, and the herring drifters, as they passed, were swept by the seas.

Night falls early these December afternoons, and soon the hills, the storm-tossed ocean, and the loch of the whooper swans were hidden in the gathering gloom.

CHAPTER VII
A Deer Forest of the West

WINTER IS late in leaving the high tops and upland glens of a Highland deer forest. Indeed, each year we seem more markedly to receive our true winter in March, April, and even May. Thus, as I write in the first week of February the air is mild, though the rain for weeks has fallen unceasingly, and even the highest hills are free of snow. Yet, in the previous May one hill road at least was impassable owing to enormous snow wreaths!

During the season of which I write, on two occasions before April was gone, summer had visited and lingered for days in the West. But as late as the last day of May the hills were freshly snow-clad, with drifts of considerable depth, so that a number of ptarmigan nests must have been snowed under.

One morning, just before this late snowfall, I was abroad upon the high tops. At 1200ft above sea level the sun shone bright and warm, the westerly breeze was soft and mild.

As I crossed a wide stretch of upland moorland where more than one hill-tarn lay, a greenshank rose from some peat hags with wild and plaintive cry. She — for I think it was the hen — quickly settled, calling anxiously. She had not, I think, commenced to lay, and a little later on I came across the cock.* He was sound asleep, perched upon one leg on a stone which rose from the placid surface of a moorland pool, and I passed on without awakening him.

In the shelter of the glen the grass was growing apace.

Beneath the cliff where a pair of peregrines were nesting, the ground was bright with primroses, while tender, soft, green fronds of the fragile oak fern grew in the shelter of the stones. The young of the falcon had hatched out — there were egg shells below the cliff — and both parents circled and sped across the face of the rock with that superb flight which is so peculiarly theirs, each calling repeatedly in harsh, grating notes pitched in different keys.

Near the head of a gloomy and unfrequented corrie, and built upon a precipitous cliff, was the eyrie of a pair of golden eagles. In it were downy young, and high above the hilltop the eagle sailed upon motionless wings, as her custom is.

From the burn side came the trilling love song of curlew — surely a sound rarely heard at an eagle's nest, for the curlew is a bird of the lower moorlands rather than of the high corries.

---

* *It is possible that grey crows, which abounded in the district, had sucked the eggs.*

Behind the eagle's eyrie rose a great hill on which the morning sun shone clearly, lighting up the big snowfields still lingering there. In the glen, close to the eagle's home, were many hinds. On the hill and far from them — for stags and hinds never feed together during summer — stags grazed upon the young grass.

It was after midday when I reached the watershed at 2500ft above sea level. The ridge was narrow and rock strewn, with steep slopes of 'scree' on either side, or sheer forbidding rocks. And when I gained this ridge I saw that the fine weather on the high hills would be of brief duration.

Away to the east all was still sunshine. South, the hills were unclouded. But west and north-west the heavens were black, and the hills of that deep blue colour which foretells a change. From the distant storm clouds the wind swept with the force of a gale, but here, away from the wind, the sun still shone warmly. As I made my way up the ridge cock ptarmigan from time to time rose just ahead of me. They flew always singly, showing that their mates had already commenced to brood their speckled eggs. Although the date was May 25th, one of the ptarmigan was still partly in his winter dress.

In places the mountain azalea — *Azalea procumbens* — was showing its flower buds of dark red. It was this year later than usual in blossoming, for the early summer had been cold, rough and sunless.

Beside a small tarn on the ridge the ground was strewn with the feathers of a hawk — perhaps the victim of a fox. Three thousand feet above the sea, and close to the hilltop, I crossed a small grassy plateau. Here were stags in numbers, young beasts, most of them, but one or two already showing their new horns. On this high plateau the grass was apparently as lifeless as in midwinter; brown and withered, and without a blade of green.

As I crossed the hilltop the storm was rapidly approaching. On Ben Nevis fleeting wisps of mist dropped momentarily, to be hurried forward upon the gale. But ever more thickly did the clouds arrive, until all the upper reaches of Scotland's highest hill were mist-shrouded. On Beinn Cruachan, on Beinn Sguliard, on Stob Choire an Albannaich the clouds, grey and persistent, were quickly descending. All view westward was obscured by rain and gloom. Yet far east, in the Ben Alder country, the sky was still cloudless.

Soon the mists were eddying around me, chill and damp.

It was not until I had dropped to near the dark loch that lies to the westward of the hill that I got beneath the mist canopy. I was now, once again, approaching the land of the curlew. Already some of the birds had hatched off their broods, and on my nearing them uttered that peculiar, agitated cry which they use when the young are abroad. A greyhen rose at my feet. Her nest, containing eight speckled eggs, was well-hidden in a clump of 'white grass'. At the water's edge a couple of common gulls were nesting.

Upon the surface of the loch, near a small, grassy island, a pair of black-throated divers swam lazily. The island seemed an ideal one for their nest, and, wading across, I quickly found the nesting hollow.

But misfortune had befallen the birds. The loch, a few days before, had risen considerably as the result of a heavy rainstorm, and the waters, troubled by the strong wind which accompanied the rain, had reached the nest and had washed out the two large and handsome eggs into the loch. Here they lay in several inches of water. And yet the nest was three feet from the edge of the loch, and the nesting place was today a good foot above the level of the water.

The tribe of the divers lay their eggs as close as possible to the water's edge — there is a Gaelic saying that the red-throated diver always nests where she can sip the water of the loch while sitting — for they are able to walk only with great difficulty, and as they progress, fall forward repeatedly. Except during their nesting season the divers never come to land — they live and sleep at sea, even in the rough weather.

As I passed down the glen beyond the loch, soft rain was falling. The grey mist fitfully rose and fell upon the hills on the breeze that had now dropped light.

On every side curlew filled the wide glen with sad music as the evening twilight crept westward, and always more heavily did the rains descend, drawing sweet perfume from the birches and fragrance from countless plants of 'roid', or sweet gale, that is so characteristic of the moorlands of the west.

CHAPTER VIII
Stulaval

SOUTH UIST is an island of contrasts. In width it averages no more than half a dozen miles, yet its seaboards, east and west, might well be a day's journey apart. Along the western, or Atlantic, side is a continuous stretch of machair, now as I write (mid-May) becoming greener with each day. Here are no hills; the wind has the same power as in mid-Atlantic, and there is no shelter of any kind.

But on the eastern seaboard, overlooking the Minch, a continuous range of hills extends along the island. There is no machair, no road even, but miles of barren, peaty moorland, with lochs, or lochans, lying in the corries and small glens. They are not high, these hills, but give the impression of being more lofty than they really are. Their plants increase the delusion. For example, the club moss (*Lycopodium selago*), which in Central Scotland is found only on the higher hills, grows in South Uist at a height of no more than 200ft above sea level.

And of a fine day the view from a thousand-foot hill in Uist equals, if it does not surpass, anything the Cairngorm giants can give.

Stulaval, some four miles north of Lochboisdale, is the highest of the hills towards the south end of the island, yet its summit is no more than 1227ft above the sea.

South Uist, as I have said, is a place of winds, and very sharp had these early May winds been during the spring of which I write. But one morning, toward the middle of the month, for the first time for many weeks, no wind stirred. The sky was soft and half-covered with high-floating cirrus clouds, giving promise of a warm day to follow. As one crossed the machair lapwings wheeled in joyous flight; northward there sped a gaggle of white-fronted geese, making toward their summer home in far-off Greenland. Although the barnacle geese left the island on April 24th, a few of the white-fronted species still remained in mid-May. It would be interesting to know what keeps them in the south after the barnacle geese have gone.

On almost every loch sandpipers twittered. They had arrived at their summer quarters but a very short time ago, for two days previously not a single one was to be seen. Like many other summer visitors, they were already paired on arrival, and at once set about searching for a nesting site. From the road at South Frobost the way to Stulaval leads first over boggy moorland, where wheatears called this May morning and cheery little twites flew in pairs. Crossing the shoulder of

Layaval (600ft), one drops down to a small, peaty burn, named on the map the Hornary River. On the south bank of this stream there is shelter from the south-west — whence come the Atlantic storms — and the heather is very long. In the most sheltered spots a few stunted willow bushes grow — now showing many golden catkins — and primroses blossom. Where a small piece of the bank of the burn had given way and had fallen half into the stream, there bloomed violets in a profusion so remarkable that they covered the grass with a continuous canopy of blue.

Although at the burn one was no more than a hundred feet above sea level, the scene was a very wild one, and might well have been 2000ft up. Not a grouse was to be seen or heard, but more curious still was the absence of curlew and golden plover. The glen was not unlike some of the high ground of the Cheviots, but had this glen been in that Border country it must have held many curlew and golden plover at this season of mid-May.

From a heathery islet on the burn a wren sang. Its song ended differently from the music of the wrens of the mainland, and the refrain persisted longer. On the islet bramble plants were budding. This was the first occasion in South Uist on which I had met with this plant, so common elsewhere, and it was curious to come across it unexpectedly on a minute island. Following up the little burn into the heart of the hills one comes suddenly upon a wide loch, by name Loch Snigisclett. It is some 250ft above sea level, and is the highest loch of any size in South Uist. Today one saw it under perfect conditions. The gentlest of breezes ruffled its peat-stained waters. Set into these dark waters there lay in the clear sunlight two grassy islets. Many gulls were nesting on them, for the loch is a remote one, and since there is no boat on it they are not molested. Lesser black-backed and herring gulls were there, and several pairs of greater black-backs. Upon one minute island there stood together two pairs of greylag geese, an eider drake and his mate, and several pairs of gulls. It is not often that one sees the eider on fresh water, but these marine ducks nest on a few of the most unfrequented lochs of Uist. Flying in from an easterly direction more geese appeared. They slanted towards the loch and alighted upon it with much splashing. Swimming up towards the islet, they clambered on to its rocky bank, being received without hostility by the birds already resting there.

High above the loch a raven sailed; a pair of hen harriers passed by. One of them 'stooped' repeatedly until almost touching the ground, then rose abruptly to repeat the same performance at intervals of a few seconds. From the loch side a steep climb brings one to the summit of Stulaval. Much of the ground is wet, and here the cotton grass (*Eriophonim vaginatum*) was flowering. The grass, and even the heather, was browned by recent gales; it seemed as though a flood had passed over the hillside, so beaten down was every plant. By the time the hilltop was reached, a keen north-west breeze had sprung up, but on the leeward side of the cairn the air was still, and in the warm sunshine one lay and admired the view on every side.

A few miles out to sea, over the Minch, the breeze seemed to die away, and the surface was glassy. Above the sea hung a soft, ethereal haze through which the great Cuchulain Hills of the Isle of Skye with their snow-splashed slopes showed dimly. Out in the Minch two trawlers were at work; just off Usinish a small boat — perhaps a lobster fisherman's craft — was slowly rounding the point. A few miles to the north was Loch Eynort, the floodtide flowing swiftly up its narrow channel, and beyond it Beinn Mhor, the chief of the South Uist hills. Southward, beyond Lochboisdale, lay the island of Eriskay, and beyond it again, Barra and its hills. West, behind the moors and the strip of green machair, lay the immense plains of the Atlantic. The Minch was untroubled by the slightest swell, but the Western Ocean appeared restless, even at this height. Along the sands the swell was breaking, and the outlying reefs were white with foam. On the north-western horizon were visible the lonely Monach Islands, peopled with a race of crofter fishermen whose dealings, even with the primitive civilization of the Outer Isles, must be few and far between. Here the swell could be seen breaking on the rocks, although the distance was close on thirty miles. On the far horizon the St Kilda group of islands showed faintly.

Immediately beneath the hill Loch Snigisclett lay, its waters appearing darker by far than when viewed close at hand. Gulls called; a pair of greylag geese browsed on the young grass of one of the islands; eiders swam quietly on the loch. A scene more peaceful was hard to visualise; yet this same loch, lying as it does in a 'pocket' amongst the hills, is in winter a place of wildest tempest, so that the water is caught up into the air and carried, on the arms of the gale, to the sea beneath. That evening the wind increased and blew yet more chill from the north, but there came on this day a new bird visitor to the island. In little companies the whimbrel, or 'May birds' arrived, considerably behind their time. They were weary and very tame, and as they rose reluctantly from their feeding, called with that curious and very distinctive note: 'tet, tet, tet, tet, tet, tet, tet'; a note which, after May is out, is heard rarely on The Long Island, but is then awakening the echoes of the hills of Iceland, where the 'lesser curlew' have their summer home.

PART II
Summer Memories

CHAPTER IX
A Western Haunt of the Ptarmigan

IN HIS recently published book, *A Hundred Years in the Highlands* the late Mr Osgood MacKenzie tells us of certain birds that are vanishing or have vanished from the North-west Highlands.

He did not mention the ptarmigan, but there is little doubt that this dweller of the high tops is yearly decreasing in the Inner Hebrides. Its enemies here are numerous, although the fox is absent. Again, from their small numbers and isolated existence, these ptarmigan of the west must now be inbred.

It is to be feared that, not so many years hence, the ptarmigan, or 'tarmachan', as it is known in Gaelic, will have become but a memory in the Inner Hebrides as it has already upon the Outer Islands, unless its enemies are kept in check and new blood is imported.

An experiment well worth the making would be to transfer a few clutches of ptarmigan's eggs from the Cairngorm hills — where the birds are numerous and healthy — to the nests of their western relatives. It would be essential that the eggs should be absolutely fresh before being packed. But I think the exchange is a possible one, and well worth trying.

Quite apart from their enemies, the ptarmigan of the West have a more trying and strenuous existence than those of their clan which dwell upon the Cairngorms. On the latter hills weeks — even months — of continuous snow and frost are experienced, but the air is dry and invigorating. Here in the West is little snow and very little frost; the birds, instead, are compelled to battle throughout the winter against gale after gale, usually accompanied by drenching sleet or rain, sweeping in from the Atlantic and eddying through even the most sheltered corries.

Recent winters have been unusually rough and wet, and I think that, even during the past five years, the ptarmigan have become noticeably fewer.

On a superb day of early June, when, after weeks of chill and blustering weather, full summer had come with a rush to the West, I landed on the shore of the Isle of Mull.

At first through woods of pine and larch the way led. Beneath the trees countless wild hyacinths bloomed, so that their scent permeated the windless air. At the edge of the woods swallows skimmed the fresh young grass, hurrying, with bills full of moist earth gathered at the edge of the tide, to their half-completed nests. Out on the open hillside a fresh breeze from Loch Linnhe moderated the heat, and curlews, hovering gracefully against the breeze, uttered their tremulous love songs. Overhead stretched away the fields of the sky, of a deep, cloudless blue – the blue of a rare summer's day when it is good to be abroad in the country of the West.

From the hill plants, growing swiftly, the warmth was drawing many scents to delight the senses. Wild orchids were there in numbers, many of the clan of the wild thyme, violets whose small blossoms rivalled the blue of the sky, and bog myrtle or sweet gale. And everywhere the health-giving scent of the heather. On the Cairngorm hills one finds the common heather or ling (*Calluna vulgaris*) up to 3300ft above the sea. But in Mull its limit seems to be about the 1500ft level, perhaps because of the more stormy conditions in the West.

Today, at a height of 2000ft, the tracks of an otter were seen in the soft peat, though no loch lay within miles, and no hill burn murmured near. But the otter is said to have a craving for frogspawn, and to wander for long distances in search of this delicacy.

At 2500ft the hilltop was reached. During the whole climb not a trace of ptarmigan had been seen, and all likely ground near the summit was carefully searched with like result.

The white grouse seemed to have left the hill.

On the large cairn marking the hilltop were many castings of the eagle. During the ascent of the hill I had seen him sail across a wide corrie, rising and falling with rhythmical movements as, leaning on the breeze, he mounted on his great wings and then, closing them, dropped gracefully earthward.

Birds of prey and owls, after a meal, disgorge the indigestible parts of their prey, and the eagle's castings were composed mainly of the fur of hares and rabbits. In one casting picked up this day was found the complete claw of a ptarmigan, the remnants of white feathers adhering to the leg showing that the bird, when devoured, had been in winter plumage. I doubt whether it is generally realised that the eagle swallows even the claws of the ptarmigan and grouse that he captures.

Far below the hilltop a wee lochan lay, reflecting in its water the intense blue of the sky. Beside it a few stags fed. They were very far back in condition, their winter coat still upon them. In the great heat they panted heavily, and one of their number, passing a peat hag, lay full length upon the semi-liquid surface, rolling from side to side with legs in air with evident relish. When he rose from his mud bath he was almost black!

Even to one knowing the hills well and the views they give, the prospect today was quite exceptional. On the southern horizon rose, hazy and scarce perceptible, the hills of the Irish coast. Nearer at hand were the heights of Arran, the conical hills of Jura, and the lonely Isle of Colonsay.

On the distant north-western horizon lay the chain of the Hebrides or the Long Island. One could distinguish Barra Head (or, as it should more correctly be named, Bernera), Mingulay with its 800-ft cliffs, and the heights above Castlebay. Then, bearing always northward, one saw the isle of Eriskay — where Prince Charles Edward Stewart made a secret landing — with its little hill. Northward still rose the big hills of South Uist — Beinn Mhor and Hekla. These Atlantic outposts were between eighty and ninety miles distant, yet their rugged slopes and the thin grey clouds that veiled their summits were clearly seen. Still farther off, and just appearing above the horizon, was the conical, though comparatively small, hill named Eaval, situated upon North Uist.

So clear was the June air, the blue serrated peaks of the Cuchulain Hills of Skye, though distant many miles, appeared near at hand.

Westward, thirty miles out into the Atlantic, lay Tiree, most delightful of islands, its long sands shining golden against the deep blue of the encircling ocean. Near it one saw Coll, and beyond that heathery isle the lonely rock of Heiskeir with its tall white lighthouse.

From east to south, hill upon hill formed the horizon. Upon Ben Nevis, their chief, a light cloud rested. The western slopes of the Ben carried little snow. Bidean nam Beann, as its Gaelic name implies, greatest of the Glen Coe hills, rose high above his fellows of that grim glen where Ossian of old had his hiding cave, and where, more recently, a very foul massacre stained the fair name of a Highland family.

Over all this wide country of hills, sun and shade pleasantly intermingled. Soft cirrus clouds, carried on the easterly breeze, moved slowly forward; away behind Skye a thunderstorm appeared to be brewing.

But, no matter in what direction one looked, the air was of an altogether exceptional clearness, and one felt the peculiar charm of the West lying over all this fair country.

At one's feet were flowering many plants of the cushion pink (*Silene acaulis*), their blooms seeming to lack something of the richness of colouring which those of the Cairngorms display. In wind-swept places one or two plants of sea-thrift were pushing up their flower buds, and among them a few plants of *Saxifraga stellaris*.

Across the hilltop was borne upon the breeze a curious scent. One could not for a time identify it — delightfully fragrant, yet somehow unexpected on the high tops. But as the breeze freshened it became more insistent, and quite unmistakable now — the aroma from the birch woods at the foot of the corrie beneath me and nearly 2000ft below! I have never known of their scent carrying thus far.

Late that afternoon I left the hilltop.

Not a single ptarmigan had been seen or heard; it seemed as though they had deserted the hill. But when I had dropped to 1900ft and had, as I thought, passed below the haunts of the white grouse, there, upon the ground at my feet, lay a ptarmigan's egg. It was cracked and deserted, but, not three feet from it, sat a ptarmigan, closely brooding upon her nest.

The forsaken egg she had, perhaps, dragged out of the nest when suddenly alarmed by the eagle.

So closely did she sit, one was able to watch her at a distance of four feet. She seemed smaller than the ptarmigan of the Cairngorms — perhaps inbreeding might account for this — and her plumage was not so richly coloured.

A pair of ravens passed silently overhead, and the ptarmigan crouched still closer upon her nest.

It was a great piece of good fortune to find, unexpectedly, one of the very few ptarmigan which had her home on the hill, for, at the outside, there could have been no more than three or four pairs. One hoped she might escape the eagle, the marauding tribe of the gulls, and the cruel and crafty grey crow.

That evening the sun sank behind the high ground in a blaze of golden light. The breeze slackened, and many birds could be seen. Terns hurried across the waters with impetuous flight, razorbills of handsome plumage and many of the tribe of the guillemot fished the deep, tide-swept stretches of the ocean.

A peculiar charm of the West is its contrasts.

Where else, within the space of an hour, can one wander at the haunt of eagle and ptarmigan, pass through woods of birches where willow warblers sing sweetly and the cuckoo throws far his soft, husky notes, and, at the tide mark, have as one's companions the oystercatcher and the clan of the sea swallows?

CHAPTER X
Loch Corodale: A Hill-set Tarn

SOUTH UIST is an island of many lochs, but of them all; the most remote must surely be Loch Corodale. The greater number of these windy lochs lie toward the Atlantic or western seaboard of the isle, where in early summer the level grazing land becomes more delightfully green with each day of mild breezes.

But with Loch Corodale it is different. So encircled by hills are its waters that they can be seen only from the peaks which surround them or from the bealach – little used nowadays, and heather-grown – that leads from Howmore across the moors to Usinish. And yet, of all the lochs of South Uist – Druidibeag with its many islands, Roag and Fada of sea trout fame, Kildonan and Ollay with fat brown trout in their waters – Loch Corodale is, perhaps, the one of most distinctive charm.

It was on a grey, hazy morning of early June that I left the road leading from Lochboisdale to Iochdar at Loch a'Phuirt Ruaidh and struck east across the desolate peat hags that extend for miles north, east, and south. How lifeless are these windy acres! Upon them scarce a living thing stirs save a wheatear or two, or a very occasional twite. One looks for a herd of stags, or an eagle, perhaps, in the distance to relieve the dreariness – but in vain.

A walk of two miles brings one to the mouth of Glen Dorchaidh, a wide glen running north-west from Beinn Mhor and holding a peat-stained burn known as the Amhuinn Beag, or, in English, the Little River. Little enough it is of a June day, but in October and November, when sheets of rain drive aslant the gale, it is a raging torrent and the big sea trout (8lb and upwards, some of them) from the Howmore River press up to its head waters to spawn.

A great fire must have swept Glen Dorchaidh and the slopes of Beinn Mhor within the past decade, for the heather has everywhere been burnt and now the glen and the hillside above it are green with the young heather shoots, a few inches high. From a boulder-strewn patch untouched by the fire a short-eared owl rose from its roosting-place and flew noiselessly up the glen. A pair of twites fluttered anxiously about their small, carefully built nest with four delicately tinted eggs.

Upon the flat summit of a high and isolated rock, perhaps 15ft high, blaeberry plants were growing in remarkable profusion. The fresh green of their young leaves was all the more pleasing and unexpected since nowhere else along the glen did they grow at all plentifully. Can it be that the Uist moors are too wet for them, or that they do not thrive upon the ground where sheep are pastured?

No crowing of grouse, no trill of curlew, broke the stillness of Glen Dorchaidh, but with laboured flight a heron passed up the burn, and a raven soared overhead, speeding downwind to a distant corrie.

Passing beneath a steep rocky slope, by name Maoladh Greag nam Fitheach, or the Ravens' Rock, one reaches the watershed at an elevation of some 1200ft above the Atlantic and all at once looks down upon Loch Corodale.

Seen from the top of the corrie this June morning the loch was very pleasing to the eye. Almost sheer from its waters, brushed by the west wind, great rocks rose south and west to a height of 1000ft.

Immediately northward was Hekla (1988ft). Only to the east was the prospect open, and here, beyond the grey waters of the Minch, one saw the Isle of Skye with its many hills, all mist-capped and hazy. Farther to the south one noted the low island of Canna. From the watershed down to Loch Corodale is not above a mile, and part of the way the track leads beside a burn. Unlike most of the moorland streams of South Uist, which are peat-stained even in the driest weather, the waters flowing to Loch Corodale are of that crystal clearness which one associates with the Dee at its source on the roof of Scotland. On this burn, for the first and only time on South Uist, I found the water ouzel nesting; behind a tiny waterfall, so far back that one could scarce peer into it, was the dome-shaped nest with its small inmates. The youngsters were less than a week old, and to find them at this early stage in June seems to show that the dipper is a much later nester on the islands than upon the mainland of Scotland. The nest was a good 100ft above the level of the loch, and the parent birds appeared to descend always to the loch for food, winging their way back with their supplies with obvious effort up the steep course of the burn. In autumn the dipper is numerous on South Uist — it is said to do much harm when the sea trout are spawning — but is very rare in summer, and I do not know that it has ever before been found nesting on the isle.

Upon a high cliff to the north of Loch Corodale a brood of ravens stood. They had left the nest, and were as capable of flight as their parents, yet they kept up an incessant croaking for food in high-pitched and querulous calls which carried far. Backwards and forwards across the face of the rock the parent birds flew, uneasy from the nearness of their hereditary enemy — man. Their deep croak mingled with the cries of their brood.

On Loch Corodale are two islands. One is large and covered with old and long heather; the other small and stony, with a few square feet of vegetation upon its highest part. Here a great black-backed gull was brooding her eggs while her mate enjoyed a bath where the waters of the burn entered the loch.

Out in the deep water a pair of red-throated divers floated. The birds were asleep, with heads tucked away beneath their feathers. Yet even in their sleep they swam forward against the breeze and soon passed out of the field of my glass.

It was pleasant to lie in a sheltered corrie after weeks of battling against the ever-present wind upon the west side of the island. The air came in puffs — now a strong breeze from the north-west, now a calm, when the loch reflected the dark rocks above it. On the ledges of these rocks the grass was fresh and green, and many wild flowers blossomed here. Primroses scented the air, the starry saxifrage opened its delicate white flowers, and everywhere the flowers of the milk wort bloomed. Of three colours — a deep blue, a rose colour, and (rarely) a pure white — the milk wort blossoms upon the hill ground of South Uist in every corrie and upon every windy slope.

In the corrie of Loch Corodale the orchids were as yet scarcely at their best, but the small red flowers of the louse wort showed above the boggy ground.

On the approach of evening dark clouds from the west kissed the gloomy summit of Beinn Mhor, rising and falling upon the black rocks. Fleeting mists just touched the cairn of Hekla also. Beyond Usinish a small boat could be seen lifting its lines; with the breeze sailed northward a herring drifter. Lowering clouds hid all distant view; the wind was backing and presaging still more unsettled weather.

Across the hill sped a peregrine falcon; low above the moorland a hen harrier quartered the ground with owl-like flight. And so dusk fell and the stillness was broken only by the murmur of the small burn and the occasional husky and far-carrying cry of a greater black-backed gull.

CHAPTER XI
Beinn Mhor of South Uist

FROM THE deep waters of the Minch, near the north end of the Isle of South Uist, three fine hills rise. Hekla, Corodale, and Beinn Mhor are their names, and of the three the greatest is Beinn Mhor (the Big Hill), reaching a height of 2034ft.

It is the highest hill in Barra or the Uists, and during the summer of which I write its summit was almost continuously hidden in mist — for the season was a sunless one and, day after day, the moisture-laden winds from the west swept across the isle. But at length, when July was a week old, came a day of clear skies and the lightest of breezes, when Beinn Mhor and its fellow hills stood out with that wonderful clearness which at times comes to the misty West. And for fairy-like beauty there is no land to compare with the country of the Hebrides when the weather is kind and the skies are clear. Yet such days are few and far between, and one must wait patiently for weeks — months, perhaps — for the conditions which make the Long Island a place of unrivalled charm.

Beinn Mhor is a hill that varies greatly, according to the position from which it is viewed. Seen from the north it presents a graceful, tapering cone. From the south it appears flat-topped and of unusual length. On its north-east face great precipices — perhaps 500ft of sheer rock — drop to dark Glen Hellisdale, yet its ascent is easy from the west and moderately easy from the south.

From the small thatched post office at Howmore the way, this July morning, led across a great 'moine', or peat moss, where many lochans reflected in their dark peaty waters the blue of the zenith. High in the air, suspended almost motionless, so it seemed, a lark sang; near him his mate fluttered from her nest with its small brown eggs in a plant of heather on a little dry knoll.

A pair of lapwings called plaintively.

Soon they and the lark were left behind, and a great silence lay upon all this wild moss and moorland.

The ascent of Beinn Mhor is very gradual and one reaches its spur — Maol Breac, 1000ft above sea level — with little effort. On such a day as this progress must be slow, for one turns frequently to admire that glorious prospect which only the western isles can give.

St Kilda, sixty miles to the north-west, grew imperceptibly and fascinatingly as one mounted. At sea level only the last 100ft of the highest hill had been visible, rising to a hazy cone just above the Atlantic horizon. Yet at 1000ft above the sea the lonely island group had become surprisingly near and distinct, and the beauty of its outline was remarkable. One could with little effort imagine how of old the visionary islesman, gazing thus from Beinn Mhor upon that ethereal island group, might imagine them to lie near to the spiritual *Tir nan Og*, or that other enchanted isle, set beyond the western horizon, known as *Rioghach Fo Thuinn*, or the Realm Beneath the Waves.

No mortal eye has seen those isles, yet here Ossian, Fionn, and other heroes dwell happily, and with them the best of the island folk of many generations.

As one gained the ridge of Beinn Mhor and looked down upon Glen Dorchaidh (the Glen of Deep Shade) and across it to Hekla and Corodale, one gazed as though upon a picture. There, through the dip between the two hills and framed by them, one saw, away beyond the unruffled Minch, the Isle of Skye about Dunvegan, with the soft summer sky blue above it.

As one reached the higher slopes of Beinn Mhor the heather gradually became more stunted and weather-beaten. At 1400ft the last unhappy-looking plant was left behind. Thus in South Uist its vertical range is less than half that on the Cairngorm hills in the central Highlands, where it grows, on the south slopes of Ben Mac Dhui, as high as 3320ft.

Not even the hardy club moss (*Lycopodium selago*) existed above 1500ft on Beinn Mhor, yet from that height up to 2000ft many violets showed their blue flowers amongst the green of the hill grass. July violets are rare. To find them one must climb to the highest and most windswept grounds. Yet on this fifth day of July the violets of Beinn Mhor were scarcely yet in full blossom. Their flower shoots are very short at such an elevation, for they are dependent upon the shelter of the scanty grass in their fight for life in this region of storms.

To the very top of the hill the blaeberry (*Vaccinium myrtillus*) extended, but nowhere did one see a single flower bud or blossom, and each leaf was deeply pigmented with reddish-brown — perhaps as a protection against the strong and cold winds which so often blow here.

The last few hundred feet of the hill — short, springy turf with a few stones scattered across it — seemed ideal ground for ptarmigan, but this bird does not nest upon any hill of South Uist, although stragglers, perhaps from Skye, occasionally are seen in autumn and winter.

There are three tops to Beinn Mhor. From the west top a very narrow, rocky ridge leads to the main top, Buail a'Ghoil, and from that again to the south top, a full mile distant, overlooking the Minch.

Of a windless summer day the way along the ridge is narrow enough. During the gusts of a winter storm it must be quite impassable.

The summit of the Beinn, when seen on a summer's day, is remarkable for its alpine flowers. No cushion pink (*Silene acaulis*) brightens the hilltop, but its place is taken by an unlooked-for plant, the sea thrift (*Armeria maritima*). During the climb one had noticed it at 1000ft, but sparingly. Now, upon the summit it was everywhere. In niches of the barren and windswept rocks, growing upon even the most exposed knolls, and in the more sheltered situations covering the ground, these flowers of varying shades of pink and red were a delight to the eye.

The sea thrift, it is true, is generally associated with the shores, yet it is found upon many of the Scottish hills, and even far inland upon the tops of the Cairngorms.

The alpine willow (*Salix herbacea*), which grows so plentifully upon the high hills of the Scottish mainland and extends towards the North Pole as far as Bear Island, grows but sparingly upon Beinn Mhor, and the soil formation is unsuited for the mountain azalea. On the slopes of the hill *Saxifraga stellaris* had been passed in flower beside the wells and small hill burns; here upon the summit it clustered about the dark rocks, its flowers weather-beaten and stunt-ed, or long-stemmed and flourishing, according as to whether they had received shelter or not.

The habitat of the plant and the appearance of its flowers on the hilltop were very different from those of this saxifrage at the lower levels, and it was not easy to recognise them as belonging to the same species. There is one characteristic, however, which unfailingly identifies the starry saxifrage (*Saxifraga stellaris*), and that is the two small spots of yellow at the base of each petal.

From the top of the hill a great buttress dropped sheer. Very grim did it seem, even upon this perfect summer day. Yet its stern aspect was softened by the flow-ers that clung precariously, so it seemed, to each minute ledge. Besides many plants of the sea thrift and starry saxifrage, the rose root (*Rhodiola rosea*) bloomed here in profusion, its golden flowers contrasting with the crimson blossoms of the sea thrift and the white fragile petals of the saxifrage, so that the great cliff formed a natural rock garden of surprising beauty. Beneath the cliff where the peregrine nests, and where, many years ago, the eagle had his home, a narrow, grassy ledge crosses the hill diagonally. Only one man, so tradition has it, has ever crossed this dangerous pass, and he was Gillespie Dubh, fleeing from his enemies in close pursuit. Thus the rocky and narrow ledge is known to this day as the Bealach, or Passage, of Gillespie Dubh. Another pass – an accessible one, this – across the shoulder of Beinn Mhor is named after one Donald Gorm.

About the hilltop the gentlest of breezes played.

At one's feet, so it seemed, lay the Minch, altogether still. Great masses of cumulus clouds – for a thunder plump was forming out to sea – were reflected in the water, so that the sea assumed unlooked-for colours, such as would have enchanted the eye of an artist. Softest greys and blues imperceptibly mingled, while away to the south the sea showed a curious and very beautiful lilac tint – such a tint as the snowy spires of distant Spitsbergen assume when seen from the cold waters of the Greenland Ocean, which bathes their lowest slopes. On the still waters of the silent Minch were curious 'lanes' leading hither and thither, caused perhaps by the faintest of airs that stirred there. Far beneath the summit of the hill a small boat from Loch Skiport moved idly near the rocky shore, the crew lifting their lobster creels. The eye saw merely a black speck upon an ethereal sea; the glass showed a boat and its busy crew of two islesmen.

At the head of Glen Hellisdale lies a small loch. Its waters were like glass, its depths black as night. From its silent shores there came, thrice repeated, the deep barking cry of a great black-backed gull, breaking the immense stillness of the hilltop. Perhaps in the days that are past, the *tarbh uisge*, or water bull, had his home here. Unlike the *each uisge*, or water horse, the water bull was generally (though not always, as witness my account of the water bull of Glen Mor Mull in another chapter) friendly toward man. This beast resembled in appearance an ordinary bull. Indeed, he mated with the cows that grazed by the shores of his loch, but his progeny might always be recognised by the expert by the shape of the ears.

Now there was once a calf born upon one of the Hebrides which, being recognised by an old woman as a young water bull, was, according to her instructions, placed in a byre by itself for seven years and fed on the milk of three cows. One day a girl herding cattle sat by the shore of a loch. To her came a strange yet comely youth, who asked her if she would 'faisg' his hair. She agreed to do him this service, so he laid his head upon her knee and she commenced to arrange his locks. But soon, to her dismay, she found growing amongst the man's hair a quantity of *liobhagach an locha*, a certain slimy weed found in lochs. Although terrified the girl continued her task without showing her fear, and when the stranger fell asleep with his head on her knee she untied her apron strings and slid the apron to the ground without awakening the sleeper. But, as she hurried homeward, she glanced behind her and her worst suspicions were confirmed when she saw him whom she had befriended pursuing her in the likeness of a horse (the water horse or *each uisge* was supposed to be able to assume human form at will). He had nearly reached her when out sprang from his shed the water bull. He rushed against the water horse, and so desperately did they fight that they entered the sea still struggling. But next day the body of the faithful water bull was cast up by the waves, all torn and disfigured by his supernatural enemy. It was said he still lived, and was brought food by the lover of the girl he had befriended, and perhaps may be alive to this day.

So much for the mythical water bull.

Today, from the cairn of Beinn Mhor even the most distant hills and islands were clear. Though it can scarce be credited, one could see, through the long glass, the white surf breaking against the rocks of St Kilda, sixty miles distant. The whitened rock ledges where countless thousands of gannets and other sea birds have their home could also be made out. And yet the distance was greater than, let us say, from London to Oxford!

How extraordinary appears that great stack a few miles north-east of the inhabited island of the St Kilda group as it rises sheer from the depths of the distant Atlantic!

Midway between Beinn Mhor and St Kilda, and perhaps thirty miles out to sea, a tank steamer steered south, rising and falling gently upon the long swell. From afar off came the boom of heavy guns, and on the distant horizon rose the smoke from unseen ships.

In the strong sunlight the sands of the low Monach Isles gleamed white; away to the north of them the island group of Haskeir, a haunt of the great grey seal, was dark and uninviting by comparison, for shade brooded there.

Full seventy miles to the northward of Beinn Mhor lie the Flannan Islands. Thus it was remarkable to see clearly not only the isles themselves, but even the lighthouse and the whitewashed wall around it.

When, in the seventeenth century, the natives of Lewis visited the Flannan Isles in summer for seabirds and their eggs, and for the down of the eider duck, they observed certain ceremonies with the greatest care – for the voyage in their small boats was a hazardous one. They would sail for the isles – about thirty miles distant – only if a breeze from the east was blowing. Should the wind change into the west before they had reached the Flannans, they would at once put about and steer for home.

Should the wind remain steady and the passage be completed in safety, the voyagers on arriving at their destination at once uncovered their heads, making a turn sun-ways and returning thanks that they had been preserved.

Sun-ways in Gaelic is *deiseil*, from *deas*, which signifies both 'right' and 'south'. For, as one faces the rising sun in the east, the fitting way to turn is toward the south (that is towards one's right). This turning sun-ways is still observed – for what piper would turn against the sun in his playing, and how important it is to pass the after-dinner port sun-ways also!

The Flannan Islands were always sacred to the people of the Lewis. On the largest island (*Eilean Mor*) were the remains of a chapel said to have been dedicated to St Flannan. When the crews of the visiting boats had reached a spot about twenty paces from the altar of this chapel they removed their upper clothes, which they laid upon a stone placed there for that purpose. They then prayed three times – the first prayer as they advanced toward the chapel on their knees, the second as they travelled sun-ways round the chapel, the third within the chapel itself. They were now free to collect seabirds' eggs and the down from the nests of the eider duck.

Another curious custom was that, no matter how many sheep might be killed on the islands, no suet might be taken back to the mainland, for such fat was regarded as sacred. Again, no bird might be killed before landing, nor might certain things on the islands be called by their proper names.

This curious custom of avoiding all reference to places by their usual names was most carefully adhered to by the islesmen of the Hebrides when they sailed abroad, in order that no evil spirit of the ocean might overhear whither they were bound. Thus no-one sailing to the Flannans ever mentioned them by name; they were known as the 'country'. In like manner the Isle of Muck might safely be named *Tir Chraine* (the Sow's Land), or the Isle of Eigg might be referred to as *Eilean nam Ban-mor* (the Isle of the Great Women), when to speak openly of them by their usual names while at sea would be to court disaster.

To view hill, sea and island from Beinn Mhor on a superb summer day is an experience worth many weeks of waiting. The sky above the Atlantic this early day of July was cloudless, yet above each island group billowy cumulus clouds hung in the windless air. They rested lightly upon the highest tops of the Cuchulain range of Skye (where, on the west-facing rocky slopes of those conical hills three winter snowfields still lingered), they kissed the hills of Rhum. Eastward, over the mainland, these clouds lay everywhere, so that the sky was grey and leaden as though presaging thunder. Yet even here the hills were distinct, and at length Ben Nevis, just over 100 miles distant, showed his snow-splashed shoulder. Distinctly, through the glass, the swell might be seen breaking upon distant Ardnamurchan Point. How incredible was it, by merely turning one's head, to see the surf upon Ardnamurchan and the surf upon St Kilda, although the two points are almost 120 miles apart!

All the hills of the Isle of Mull — Beinn Mor, Beinn Talaidh, Dun da Ghaoith — showed clear, and just above the Isle of Coll one saw the higher points of the far-off Treshnish Islands — the flat top of Lunga and the rounded cone of Bac Mor, or the Dutchman. Beyond them again could be viewed the little hill of Iona — Dun I, by name. Upon Tiree, a full fifty miles away, each house showed distinctly. West of them, and far out to sea, the tall lighthouse of Skerryvore, sixty miles distant, appeared needle-like against the horizon.

Ardnamurehan, Skerryvore, Monach, Heiskeir, the Flannan lighthouse — have all these lighthouses ever before been visible at the same moment? Certainly only from a hilltop and in weather which comes but rarely, even in summer.

For three hours we remained, this superb day, upon the summit of Beinn Mhor. Around the precipices or high overhead ravens soared, their deep croak clear in the silence of the hills.

Sheep fed right up to the hilltop, and even rabbits climbed thus far for the tender hill grass.

Around the eastern top of the hill the ground is peaty — peats were cut here for the great bonfire that was lighted one misty night to celebrate the coronation of King Edward VII —and even at this height the butterwort (*Pinguicula*) grew, though its flower buds were as yet scarcely showing.

Late that afternoon a great cloud formed above Beinn Mhor. It grew black as night above the hilltop, though a few miles to the west the sun still shone bright-ly. Soon the rain storm broke. From the fringe of the cloud, some miles out over the Minch, thunder-rain descended. It hid the hills of Skye, it rendered hazy and indistinct the mountains of the distant mainland; but upon Beinn Mhor itself the rain did not fall. With the passing of the shower the air became, if possible, yet more incredibly clear, and when, after ten o'clock that evening, the sun sank behind the Atlantic in a cloudless sky, the hills, lochs, and islands — distant and near at hand — were bathed in a soft, warm glow.

But with morning came a hard and cold north wind that swept across Beinn Mhor and its attendant hills.

Gone were the stillness and peculiar charm of the preceding day, yet in the mind's eye that charm is retained and stored as a priceless gift which only the West in her fairest mood can give.

CHAPTER XII
Summer Shielings

BORDERING THE Atlantic there lies, throughout the length of South Uist from Polachar to Iochdar, a strip of fertile machair land. In April this machair is browned and withered by the bitter, salt-laden winds; it is lifeless as the tundra of the Arctic regions on the melting of the snows, yet by June it is bright with a multitude of wild flowers. Here grow the beautiful *Orchis incarnata*, with flower heads of deep crimson, and amongst it the sweet scented *Orchis maculata*.

One finds, too, the wild pansy (*Viola tricolor*), the bird's-foot trefoil (*Lotus corniculatus*) with masses of golden bloom, and the centaury (*Erythræa*).

Here and there the purple flower heads of the knapweed rise above the surrounding herbage. The Latin name of this plant, *Centaurea*, is from the Centaur Chiron, who is said to have healed wounds with it. Then there are the harebell, with delicate pendulous flowers, the silver weed with its silvery leaves and golden blossoms, the wild thyme, vipers' bugloss, the common bugle, and many other charming plants.

Here the dunlins speed with arrow-swift flight, the lapwings wheel and scream, and the greylag geese feed of an evening.

But beyond the machair is a great expanse of desolate moorland, with a multitude of lochs and lochans, peat hags, and, beyond all these, a chain of storm-scarred hills.

This country of moorland and hills is now deserted and entirely lonely except for an occasional shepherd gathering in his sheep, but less than half a century ago not a few summer shielings were here. Far up Glen Dorchaidh or upon the lower slopes of Stulaval one sees, contrasting vividly with its sombre surroundings, a flaming patch of 'seilisdeir' or yellow iris. And seeing this, one knows that here was once a summer shieling — for the seilisdeir grows not upon the open moor except where a human habitation once stood. And always about the patch of iris the ruins of the shieling can be seen. Some of these ruins are scarce visible, others are surprisingly well-preserved — but all are now deserted, for the day of the summer shieling is past and will no more return.

It must have been a sorrowful day for the crofters when they abandoned their primitive summer homes upon the windswept moorlands.

With what pleasure was the journey to the summer shieling prepared for! There was impatient waiting for the mountain pastures to become green, so that the sheep and cattle could be driven to the hills. How eager must the children have been for their summer home! Even the old people must have looked forward to the change.

But these times are no more, and the cattle are pastured in summer on the machair, and the crofters live in their permanent home throughout the year, journeying to the moorland only to cut and carry their peats, or to cut long heather for the dyeing of their tweed.

It is the same throughout the Highlands and Islands. Of the summer shielings that were everywhere – in Lochaber, in Rothiemurchus, upon the mainland of Argyll – not one remains in use; but in South Uist it is not only the land of the summer shielings that is now dreary and desolate. Along the eastern coast of the island one sees many deserted crofts. No summer shielings are these, but dwellings that were lived in from one year's end to another.

The small ridged fields, tilled by the hand plough, known as the 'cas chrom', are still visible. They are small, it is true, but on them oats and potatoes were grown. They are now for many years derelict and grass-grown, and there is but a single family – that of a shepherd – along the whole of the eastern seaboard from Loch Eynort to Loch Skiport.

No road leads across to that lonely dwelling of the Gaelic-speaking shepherd, but one may cross to it by way of more than one mountain pass, or along a wild and rocky track from the shore of Loch Skiport.

How different is this eastern coast of Uist from the west side of the isle, with its fertility and its flatness! Deep glens dip abruptly to the waters of the Minch. Through each of these glens a hill stream hurries, with white waterfalls. Many of these hill burns enter the sea in a long gleaming cascade, the roar of which mingles with the boom of the surf upon the rocks.

Although the eastern side of South Uist is now deserted, it is less storm-swept than the western shores, with their many crofting communities, for Hekla, Beinn Mhor, and many lesser hills give protection from the south-west gales. And the glens slope southward and so catch the sunlight. Lack of roads has been the cause of this desertion of the eastern side of Uist. In the little bays terns fish of a summer's afternoon and oystercatchers pipe, proclaiming to all by their oft-repeated call, 'gille Brighid, gille Brighid', that they are the servants of St Bride of the Shores.

Across the Minch, Skye seems at hand when the weather is clear, and in the grim corries of the Cuchulain Hills lingering snowfields can be seen up to the end of July. Skye, Rhum, Carina, Ardnamurchan, even the distant Isle of Mull itself, might be viewed from these crofts, now in ruins. Curiously enough, when I descended to one of these ruins from a high bealach one soft and humid day of July, I saw a couple of song thrushes leave them. They were Hebridean song thrushes, now held to be distinct from their relatives of the mainland, and I thought they might be nesting. Since there are no trees in Uist, the thrushes — and there are not many of them — nest in the cranny of a wall or in a cleft of rock. Perhaps, if they are fortunate, they may find a gorse bush, or make their nest in one of the rhododendron bushes which have been planted sparingly through the isle.

It was curious and unexpected to see the thrushes in that ruined dwelling, for, so desolate has this eastern coast of South Uist become, a shepherd living beside remote Loch Corodale has recently moved his home to the western side of the isle, for even he could not stand the long winter nights in his solitary glen, where the wind came in such fierce gusts from off the hills that his roof threatened to be torn bodily heaven-ward.

Yet, in summer at least, this eastern coast is a pleasant place. On the hillsides the bell-heather blossoms. With it the blue milkwort, the golden bog asphodel, the white grass of Parnassus, blend their colours, and in sheltered ravines fox-gloves and the royal fern (*Osmunda*) grow. I have said that no tree grows upon South Uist. Yet that is not strictly correct, for there are trees, though one might be abroad upon the isle for days without seeing them, and in no ease do they reach the height of a tree upon the mainland or even the Inner Hebrides. Upon the banks of the lochans — wherever it can find shelter from the incessant storms — the rowan or mountain ash grows in bush-like form. In the deep gorges the aspen shakes its quivering leaves, but it is a rare tree on South Uist.

The aspen, it is said in the West, was the tree that supplied the wood for the cross of Christ. Its remorse has ever since been so great that its leaves constantly tremble, even when the faintest air stirs.

One day of early summer I crossed the island to the eastern coast, making my way by the pass that rises from peat-stained Loch Spotal, and heather-clad Coire na h'Eitich to the watershed. Here a large cairn of stones marks the little-used track, for many funerals must have passed here, and it was the custom, wherever the coffin was rested, for each of the mourners to put a stone on that place. In the corrie the sun had shone warmly, for the steep slopes of Hekla gave shelter, but on the ridge the wind blew from the south with the force of half a gale.

About the loch beneath greylag geese flew with querulous cries. From some long heather a short-eared owl rose silently and winged its way with curious ghost-ly flight across the loch.

Overhead a pair of hen harriers circled — the male very handsome in his light slate-coloured plumage, the hen dark brown and buzzard-like. Amongst the rocks ravens croaked and grey crows called harshly.

Yet one missed the trilling of the curlew, the tuneful pipe of the 'feadag' or gold-en plover, the plaintive song of the ring ouzel — for the moorlands of South Uist know none of these birds.

At first the sky was blue and only the lightest of mists rose and fell upon Hekla's top. But when I had crossed the pass and had made my way along the east side of the island to where I looked across to gloomy Loch Corodale, the weather was quickly changing. From the south dark clouds were hurrying up. They shrouded the hills, they gradually crept lower.

Soon all the land almost to sea level was wrapped in an impenetrable mist-curtain and a drizzling rain commenced to fall. Descending to a lower level, I set a course for the solitary shepherd's house at Usinish, for I knew that from here a track would lead me back along the coast to Loch Skiport.

The shepherd's wife was at her washing by the burn. The visit, even of an islander, is a very rare event with her; the sudden appearance of a stranger must have been doubly surprising. But, with that hospitality which is so characteristic of the West, she bade me welcome in her soft Gaelic, and insisted that I should enter and take a cup of tea before proceeding on my way. The rain descended more heavily and persistently, and even with her son to guide me I found the track from her house to the west side of the island a difficult thing to follow, with bogs and rocks and innumerable burns to cross.

And if it were a path hard to see on an early summer's day what must it be of a winter's night, when the gale carries in its arms wild squalls of sleet and rain, and when in the darkness the track, even at one's feet, is invisible?

Is it to be wondered at that all the islanders, save one family, have left the eastern coast of this lonely island?

CHAPTER XIII
A Uist Headland

AT TWO points on the eastern side the Atlantic bites deeply into South Uist. Near th e centre of the isle Loch Eynort winds far inland with sinuous course; farther southwards Loch Boisdale, eating its way westward, forms a broad peninsula of the southern part of the island.

This peninsula is a place of rugged moorland and heathery hills, and is uninhabited in its central and eastern parts.

The highest hill in this portion of the island is Easaval, some 800ft above the sea; but there are a number of hills of more than 500ft, with peat hags lying in between them, and lochs, with grassy or heather-clad islands upon them, in many of the hollows of the land.

On a July day, warm and with most brilliant sunshine, when first I crossed this lonely country, each loch and tarn was reflecting the azure blue of the sky, and the air was redolent with the scent of innumerable bog-myrtle plants.

Upon South Uist the 'roid' or bog myrtle is not common, and it is only upon the southern peninsula of the isle that it grows in profusion. Elsewhere I have seen it only in sheltered spots along the margin of some loch. It may be that the level mossy 'flats' are too windswept for its requirements.

Standing upon the shoulder of Easaval, one looks across the crofts of South Lochboisdale to the grassy isles known as Eilean an Iasgaich. Beyond these, again, and across the loch, is the village of Lochboisdale, with the tall mast of the wireless station a prominent landmark.

But though one looks upon crofts in plenty in the distance, the land near at hand is rugged and uninhabited.

Here, amongst long heather and bracken of vivid green, a merlin called anxiously. Its nest must have been concealed in the heather, but time did not permit of a search being made. This dashing little hawk is not common in Uist, nor is its relative, the kestrel, met with except occasionally. The alarm note of the merlin when its nesting ground is approached is curiously reminiscent of a turnstone's cry, as I heard it upon the nesting isle of a pair of those birds on the northwest coast of Spitsbergen. It is a succession of short, sharp, whistling notes, pitched very high, and rapidly repeated.

Near the merlin's nesting site the hillside had evidently been fired recently, for the heather was browned and the bracken singed and drooping at the edge of the blackened patch. A burnt hill face is never artistic. In spring its scent is attractive. In mid-July it is incongruous, and the burnt area an eyesore. In the long heather, and away from the breeze, the heat was intense, and for the first time that summer 'clegs' (the name of the stealthy horsefly, with a painful bite) put in their appearance in full force. There is a saying in the West that in July the cleg is in possession of both eyes; in August it loses one! Certain it is that on the day of which I write the troublesome insects had the sight of both their eyes unimpaired!

It was well on in the afternoon before I reached the most outlying headland. It is given on the map as Ru (or Rudha) Melvick, and its height is 487ft. From the sun-baked hilltop one looked almost sheer into the sea below. The last of the breeze had died away. Pale green were the waters near the shore, for the white sand shone through them, but farther out their colour was a deep blue. During the earlier part of the day one had caught fleeting glimpses of the sea, and had noted far out in the Minch, between Tiree and Barra, a large four-masted sailing barque making her way slowly northward. But now that the southerly breeze, before which she sailed, had died away, she lay there becalmed, with all her sails set — a strikingly picturesque object in the great expanse of waters.

From the rocks many gulls flew with querulous cries backwards and forwards far below me. Just above the emerald waters an oystercatcher winged its way. This brightly coloured bird has a curiously beautiful legend attached to itself, for it is known to the islesmen as *Gille Brighid* or St Bride's servant. St Bride or Brighid of the Shores, called sometimes the Fair Woman of February, in the folklore of the Gaels is mentioned as Christ's foster-mother. His mother Mary was a sweet influence in the daily lives of the islanders, but of his foster-mother there was no mention in the Good Book, and since to the Gaelic mind it was incredible that even a chieftain, much less a king, should be without a foster-mother, St Bride was chosen.

Why, then, is the oystercatcher known as St Bride's bird, it may be asked? It is for a service which it rendered the Christ, when He, sitting upon a sea-washed rock, was in danger of His enemies, hurrying toward Him through the bealach. They quickly approached, and just as it seemed they must spy the wanderer, an oystercatcher flying up covered its Lord with sea tangle. Because of this act of devotion, St Bride made it her own bird.

Beyond Mull and Ardnamurchan, when the sun shone clear, great thunder-clouds were piled up, this July day, above the Appin and Lochaber districts; but south and west the sky was blue, with a line of fleecy cumulus clouds above the far distant Irish coast.

Northward one looked across the three big hills of Uist — Beinn Mhor, Hekla, and Corodale — to the birthplace of Flora Macdonald, the heroine of Prince Charles Edward's escape from the isles.

Upon the short heather and rocks the sun shone with great heat. Already the bell-heather — much later in flowering in the West than in Central Scotland — was budding, and in the wetter ground the flowers of the bog aspodel were opening.

In Uist there are no lizards to bask upon sun-warmed hill slopes, no adders to hiss angrily at the intruder. The stoat is absent and even the frog.

Upon the heather no honeybees search for honey, nor does one see them upon the clover and other sweet-smelling flowers of the fertile machair land. The bumblebee is present, but is not numerous.

I have said that no houses or crofts stand upon this lonely headland, yet it was peopled today with sturdy men and women from the island of Eriskay across the Sound, who had taken advantage of the warm sunshine and calm sea to sail across in their boats and carry the peats they had dug from the moss west of the headland. Bronzed fisher folk, most of them, their knowledge of the English tongue was slight. About the peat moss, blue smoke was rising from the fires on which the refreshing tea was being brewed, for it was strenuous work carrying sackfuls of peat from a height of several hundred feet down to sea level. In the little bay of Eriskay lay a fleet of herring craft, for the day was Saturday, and the boats had come in from Castlebay for the weekend rest. In the Sound, solan geese from their distant nesting grounds at St Kilda fished untiringly. Corn buntings twittered in the fields about Polachar. Late that afternoon the wind, which had been southerly before the calm fell, came away from the north-west, following the sun, and seeming to give promise of a spell of more settled weather than had been the lot of the Western Isles during that summer.

PART III
Autumn, Winter and other Memories

CHAPTER XIV
The Fish of the Howmore

SOUTH UIST is a remote isle, and even in summer the crossing of the Minch is usually a stern test of the sailing qualities of the most robust.

The steamers are small and surprisingly lively, and even when the weather is kind and the sun shines brightly there is often a long Atlantic 'roll' sweeping in with great power from the open spaces of the ocean. Yet on a day of calm nothing can be more delightful than the six hours' sail from Mallaig to the South Uist harbour of Lochboisdale.

There is first a call at the small island of Eigg. The desolate and mountainous island of Rhum, with its wide green corries through which flow glistening streams, is next visited, and, after a few minutes' stop at the adjoining Isle of Canna, the small mailboat sets her course for Lochboisdale. As the islands recede and the ocean 'heave' begins to be felt, raven, buzzard, cormorant, and oyster-catcher are left behind; and now there circle round the steamer with superb flight, graceful fulmar petrels, those true birds of the ocean which never approach land except during the season of their nesting.

Gradually, right ahead, the dim outline of the hills of South Uist – Beinn Mhor, Corodale, Stulaval – become more distinct, until, shortly after eight in the evening, Lochboisdale is reached. As the steamer approaches the pier the whole of the population of the village seems there to welcome it, yet one hears not a word of English – the talk is all in Gaelic.

Here upon the remote island of South Uist is Howmore, of fishing fame. Though not many anglers have fished the Howmore waters, there are few who have not heard of them; indeed, their renown has become almost proverbial.

About twelve miles north of the small harbour of Lochboisdale are the big hills of the island. The birthplace of the Howmore (or, as it should more properly be written, *Hough Mor*) River is amongst these wild hills. Yet the river itself is considerably less than a mile in length, and its tributaries which extend to the hills give the river what water it has. Following up the main Howmore River for this short mile, one comes unexpectedly upon a peat-stained loch with stony shores – Loch Roag by name.

Into this loch two burns flow. One, coming from the east, rises beyond a hill loch – Loch Airidh Aulaidh – but need not be mentioned further, as it is impassable to the salmon and sea trout until late in October by reason of an iron grating placed across the burn where it enters Loch Roag. Flowing into Loch Roag from the south is another, very short, burn coming from Loch Fada (the Long Loch), and as this burn is left open the fish crowd through it into Loch Fada. Here they must remain, until the end of the fishing at all events, for an iron grating prevents their entering the burn at the head of that loch. The Howmore water, then, consists properly of the river itself and the two lochs, Roag and Fada.

But, not more than a couple of hundred yards from the seashore, a branch of the river breaks away in a north-easterly direction. Sea trout running up this branch enter the schoolhouse lochs and Loch an Eilean (the Loch of the Island), and would press on into the large moorland loch, Druidibeag, were they not held back by an iron grating, for Loch Druidibeag is considered to be too large and windswept to be fished with the best results. And how different is the water of these two branches of the Howmore River! That flowing from Loch Roag is peat-stained, even after weeks of dry weather, while that from Loch an Eilean is always clear. Although the Howmore River and lochs are famous chiefly for their sea trout, they hold a certain number of grilse and salmon also, but they are not easy to 'move' with the fly – the only lure permissible in these waters.

There are two runs of sea trout. In spring there is a short season from the middle of March till mid-April. No salmon enter the river at that time, but there are heavy sea trout up to and exceeding 8lb in weight. But it has always been a debated point whether these sea trout are true clean-run fish or merely well-mended kelts. Be this as it may, by mid-April the sea trout have all returned to the sea, and it is not until the last week of June that the first summer fish commence to enter the river. The earliest running fish are not sea trout, but grilse and salmon, and July is well-advanced before the first run of sea trout enter the fresh water. It is during August and September that the big sea trout arrive. In the Howmore they are of unusual size; fish of 7lb to 8lb are numerous, and monsters of 15 to 16lb have been known. Fresh-run sea trout continue to come in from the sea right up to the closing day of the fishing (October 31st), and excellent sport is often obtained during the first fortnight of October, but towards the end of the fishing the sea trout become dark and heavy with spawn, and rapidly fall off in condition. Yet one which my wife hooked in late October in Loch Fada gave an exciting run of an hour and a half before it could be netted.

Although the lochs hold many more fish than the Howmore River, the fishing of the river gives greater enjoyment. At low tide the stream runs over several hundred yards of sand. The peaty water extends to a considerable distance out to sea, and where it enters the salt water the river is turbid from the particles of fine sand in suspension. Along the tide stand rows of ponderous great black-backed gulls, and off the river mouth a seal, perhaps, swims on the lookout for fish.

There are pools through this sandy stretch, but they frequently change their size and shape and are usually half-blocked by a forest of broken stems of 'tangle' or laminarian seaweed. These stems have been dislodged by the prevalent winds from the south-west, and their disintegrating remains have a very distinctive, though not altogether unpleasant, smell. These pools produce an occasional sea trout, but the fish generally run straight through to the Bridge Pool. This is the best pool in the river, and is rarely without one or two heavy fish. But even the Bridge Pool frequently changes its formation, and that part immediately above the bridge is often filled in with sand, which it takes a strong floodtide or heavy spate to dislodge. From the Bridge Pool for a couple of hundred yards are shady shallows. Then comes a small deep pool (usually productive of little), and the river above this consists of a succession of long, still pools, between flat, short-cropped banks of grass and sea thrift.

During one season the first fish were observed in the Bridge Pool on the last Sunday of June. They were salmon of perhaps 8lb to 12lb in weight, and were lying near the bridge, from which they could be seen without much difficulty. These fish soon passed up the river into the lochs, and it was not until close upon mid-July that a second run of fish entered the pool.

The Bridge Pool is not easy to fish, and the water must be in just the right state for the salmon to take the fly. Most tides enter this pool, and it is useless to fish after the arrival of the salt water, and one must wait until the salt and brackish water has left the pool before throwing a line. If the volume of fresh water be too large the fish do not take; again, if there be too little water they see the angler and his line. Thus there are very few days when the Bridge Pool is in good order.

On July 12th, I walked by way of the shore from Grogary Lodge to the Howmore River, a distance of just three miles. A good breeze was blowing from the west in the early part of the day, but before I had reached my destination this had died away to the gentlest of airs, and the surface of the Bridge Pool was unruffled. Concealing myself upon the bridge, I paid out line gradually into the deep water below me. The fly – a small 'blue charm' – showed up well, but so bright was the sun and so still the water the line and the cast were clearly visible. It was most interesting to watch the effect of the fly as it floated down, with gentle, jerky movement to give it an appearance of vitality, to where the fish were lying. One old salmon was constrained, each time the fly came over him, to rise from his 'lie' in deep water and have a look at it. A grilse also came very near to taking it, but contented himself with 'nosing' it and a little later springing high out of the water.

The fact that the fish showed an interest in my fly on so unsuitable a day gave me hopes, and on July 14th I returned to the Bridge Pool. The morning was quiet, though dull. Along the shore lesser terns were endeavouring to hatch out belated clutches of eggs – for they had suffered much from the attentions of marauding common gulls – and ravens searched the sands for any tasty trifle thrown up by the surf. Around the Bridge Pool a pair of rock pipits flew. They were anxious for their young brood, now almost full-fledged, which were concealed in a cranny of the masonry of the bridge.

Along the river banks the oats were green and full of growth — the season was a very late one — and the potatoes, backward, but now making headway fast, were being cleaned and hoed by the crofters. Above the fields larks still sang, and corn buntings nested among the growing crops, from which came the 'crek, crek' of the landrail.

Now, for the fishing of the Bridge Pool it is important that the greater volume of water should come from the Loch an Eilean branch of the river, for as I have said, the main stream is peaty and slightly brackish, while the water of the tributary is clear and sweet, and entirely fresh. The two streams meet so near the Bridge Pool that one side of the pool sometimes may be clear while the other is peat-stain.

On this occasion the clear water predominated, for the Loch an Eilean tributary, coming from the large Loch Druidibeag, had stored up the heavy rains of the previous week. Before I had commenced to fish the pool the sun had broken through the clouds, and, so clear and calm was the water, it was obviously useless to fish from the banks. From the bridge two nice grilse could be seen lying almost below the structure. These I stalked with great care, and, lying behind the grassy wall held the rod above the stream and gradually paid out line. As the small 'silver doctor' fly dropped down to where the grilse were lying, one of them rose slightly from the bottom and examined it, but with little interest. I kept the fly above the fish, moving it gently past them and then allowing it to drift down to a few yards below them. This I did constantly for just twenty minutes. One of the grilse from time to time rose as though to take the fly, but thought better of it. Then, after twenty minutes, he suddenly seized the fly, hooking himself firmly. It was extraordinarily interesting, for the whole of the twenty minutes I had been watching the fish at close quarters, and it was an exciting moment to see him take the fly truly and well, and difficult for me not to 'strike' prematurely. Having hooked the fish, it was necessary to jump from the bridge down to the sand below. He played well, but never seemed to recover from his surprise at being hooked. His weight was 4lb, and he was quite fresh run, with sea lice upon him.

Three days later (July 17th), on a close and thundery day, I fished the Bridge Pool without success. In that part of the pool lying just above the bridge a large shoal of sea trout were swimming. They were at the neck of the pool, and apparently were anxious to ascend the river, but there was little water at the time. They were small fish of the finnock type, the largest perhaps a pound and a half in weight.

A week later — a day of clear skies with a strong northerly breeze blowing — the Bridge Pool was a different place to fish, for the wind was blowing against the current. Early in the afternoon I touched what seemed to be a big fish, and, returning to the pool in the early evening, almost at my first cast a salmon took the fly not more than three yards from where I was standing. The strong breeze was causing the line to 'belly' at the time, and from the first I was doubtful if the fish was well-hooked; indeed, I had a horrid suspicion that he would escape. The salmon played well, but at the end of half an hour he was tired out, and I steered him into the edge of the pool. Another minute would have seen him ashore, but at the critical moment the fly lost its hold, and the fish, after remaining for a second or two in a dazed state, swam slowly and tantalizingly back into the peaty depths.

One night in mid-July I shall always remember. It was about nine o'clock when I visited the Howmore River. The spring tide that evening had been unusually high. It had invaded the whole of the river, entered Loch Roag, and continued into Loch Fada beyond it. When I arrived the tide was on the turn, and a heavy volume of water — mostly salt — was hurrying seaward through the Bridge Pool, which, of course, was bank-high. The pool was literally alive with grilse and salmon, and they appeared half-mad with excitement. Fish after fish leapt high above the water's surface — beautiful silvery fish they were — so that the small pool was a place of confused and turbulent water from the constant leaping of grilse and salmon. After a time the salmon quietened down, and as the tide receded and the pool gradually shrank to its normal dimensions not a fish showed. Nor would they look at a fly a little later on, when I fished the pool carefully.

I have written much of the Bridge Pool, to the exclusion of the rest of the river, but I have done so as in my opinion this pool is incomparably the best. The long succession of deep and quiet pools near the head of the river are monotonous fishing unless fish be rising freely — and they never did rise at all during the July of which I write.

Years ago a grating used to be placed across the Howmore River just below where it leaves Loch Roag. This grating was kept there till late in the season, forcing the fish to remain in the river instead of entering the lochs. This plan was discontinued owing to the fact that in a dry summer the river shrank to such an extent that its water became tepid from the warm sun, and almost stagnant, so that the fish became sluggish and lost condition. But in a season such as 1922 it would seem good policy to have a grating in use until, let us say, the end of July.

Salmon and grilse never take freely in the Howmore lochs, and latterly have been more difficult than ever to catch, whereas in the river, under suitable conditions, they rise to the fly. Quite apart from this, river fishing, to my way of thinking, is infinitely preferable to sitting all day in a boat without knowing where, exactly, the fish are lying. At present most grilse and sea trout run right through the river in the course of an hour or so, and the only indication of their passing is the 'bow wave' which they throw up as they cross the shallows. Thus, when fishing conditions are at their best, the river may be empty, or almost so, of fish. Were these salmon kept in the river for, say, a month, they would not have time to go back in condition, and, should the river become too low, the barrier could always be removed.

Howmore is far, very far, off the beaten track, and in this lies much of its charm. Its three sentinel hills — Hekla, Beinn Mhor, and Corodale — are ever in sight of the angler. On the river banks stand the small thatched cottages of the Gaelic-speaking island crofters, whose ducks swim happily in the pools. In fine weather it is a delightful country, but of late years fine weather has come rarely to the West, and more often than not a south-westerly gale sweeps across the machair and the river beside it, while the hills are hidden in driving mists.

CHAPTER XV
Hekla: A Peak of South Uist

FOR WEEKS wild weather had prevailed among the Western Isles. Day after day the wind had blown strong – often with gale force – the driving mists were low on the hills, rain fell aslant the gale.

Then one day (it was October 23rd) the wind dropped, the air cleared, and that superb weather which one finds only in the Hebrides, and even there but rarely, brought under its influence the whole of the Long Island.

In South Uist the two greatest hills are Beinn Mhor (2034ft) and Hekla (1988ft). No great heights are these when compared with the Cairngorms or Ben Nevis, yet from the summit of Hekla, this October day, was as fine and varied a view as from Ben Nevis itself.

From the lodge at Grogary the way led southward as far as the village of Howmore. Here the road was left, and one walked for miles through moorland bogs, where some of the peat still lay ungathered, to the slopes of Helda.

Grouse have decreased in South Uist of recent years – as, indeed, throughout all the Outer and Inner Hebrides – but this sunny morning one saw quite a number of the brown birds. Has it ever been remarked that the grouse of the Outer Hebrides have a more subdued cry when alarmed than the birds of the central Scottish moors? There seems to be little doubt that this is really the case.

In the bogs snipe crouched low, rising at one's feet with rasping cry. Along the course of the peaty Amhuinn Beag (the Little River) one was sheltered from the slight easterly breeze, and the sun, though low in the sky, shone with almost summer heat. All the western side of South Uist consists of low, level ground. Near the Atlantic it is grazing land; farther inland it isa country of lochs, lochans, and peat hags. Thus Grogary is no more than 20ft above sea level, and Howmore scarcely as much.

Following the course of the Amhuinn Beag, one came to a remote hill loch – Loch Airidh Aulaidh – and now one looked away up Glen Dorchaidh to where the stream has its birth in the corries of Beinn Mhor. Even thus far do the celebrated sea trout of the Howmore River penetrate when, in late October, the gratings are removed from Loch Roag and the fish, with the first spate, press upward to spawn. At the head of Glen Dorchaidh stand Beinn Mhor and Corodale, on the rocky slopes of which the raven has his home.

Curiously enough, during the whole of this October morning, a dark cumulus cloud rested above Beinn Mhor, so that the hill was constantly in deep shadow, while on Hekla the sun shone uninterruptedly.

At 1000ft the crowberry, the club moss, and the alpine willow were sparingly on the hill. This willow (*Salix herbacea*) on the Cairngorms is never met with much below 3000ft, but in the Hebrides the vertical range of all alpine plants is much lower than in central Scotland. I once found *Salix herbacea* on the slope of Hekla above Loch Druidibeag little more than 300ft above sea level.

As one climbed, one gradually came to realise the unusual clearness of the air and the extent and beauty of the view. Far out upon the placid waters of the Atlantic rose the St Kilda group of isles. Upon the largest of them — Hirta, or the west-lying isle — which alone of the group is inhabited, a shower of rain was descending, and through the glass one could see the mist rise and fall upon the hilltop. But on Boreray, a few miles north-east, where is the largest colony of solan geese in British waters, the sun shone clear, lighting up the great cliffs.

The appearance of this precipitous island — with the lesser rock of Stac an Armin beside it — rising sharply from the horizon with tapering pinnacles, reminded one strangely of the hills of Prince Charles Foreland, west of the Spitsbergen coast, as one saw them for the first time when approaching that Polar archipelago. This great stack lies alone in vast Atlantic solitudes; the nearest land is Harris, and that is a full fifty miles distant.

During the war, German submarines, after their passage north of Scotland (they usually took that route, since the English Channel was heavily mined), used often to take their bearings from St Kilda. The coastguard, temporarily established here, were able in clear weather to pick up these hostile vessels at a very great distance, and by wireless promptly passed on this intelligence to the patrols and the admiral commanding at Stornoway. Then one day there appeared a submarine which commenced to bombard the island, aiming at the wireless station. In this the enemy were perfectly justified, and the islanders, terrified out of their lives, took to the hill. The wireless station was wrecked, and, since there was no gun to guard it, the men in charge were helpless.

To return to Hekla. At some 1200ft above sea level one noticed a most interesting thing — the arrival, from a great height, of a large flock of redwings. They had evidently just come in from the sea, and it is not often that one sees them complete their overseas flight.

Climbing by the ridge of Hekla one looks, to the south'ard, into that dark glen by name Glen Usinish, at the head of which lies hill-girt and remote Loch Corodale. Surely, if anywhere, the *each uisge*, or supernatural water horse, still has his home here; so encircled by big hills is the loch that the low October sun is able to shine upon it for a few minutes in the morning only. The water horse assumes many shapes; he often appears as a man, and sometimes as a large bird.

A certain West Highlander once had the good fortune to see the *each uisge* in its feathered shape. In form and colour the supernatural being was very like a great northern diver, with the exception of the white upon its neck and breast. Its neck was no less than 2ft 11in long and 23in in circumference!* The bill was 17in long, hooked like an eagle's at the end. The feet had enormous claws. The foot-prints, seen on the shores of the loch, were larger than those of an elephant!

It is possible the narrator mistook the bird-monster he saw, and that it was really none other than the gigantic mythical water bird called the 'boobrie'. Now the boobrie was supposed to inhabit the freshwater and sea lochs of Argyllshire. He was a gigantic bird, with a ravenous appetite, devoured sheep and cows, and possessed a very loud hoarse voice. He was obviously an evil creature, for he on one occasion terrified a minister out of his senses!

Suddenly among the redwings above Loch Corodale a strange restlessness was apparent; from the hillside they rose hurriedly. The cause of their alarm was soon visible, for a hen harrier with graceful and leisurely flight appeared above the hill-side.

What a picture for a Thorburn – the black loch in grim shadow far below, the sunny slope above which the affrighted redwings moved uncertainly, the blue-plumaged harrier soaring easily, with wings held V-shape.

The summit of Hekla was gained an hour after midday. Here are great rocks with white quartz veins running through them, set on a narrow ridge. A place where all the four winds are free to roam at will. Yet today scarce a breath of air stirred and overhead from afar came the deep croak of a wandering raven.

And what an altogether glorious view lay on every side! One doubts the power of any pen to describe it.

Hills at an incredible distance were clear.

A little to the east of south the mountains of Mull stood out against the cloud-less horizon. Of these hills the most distant from Hekla is Duin da Ghaoith, which rises from behind Torosay, not ten miles from Oban. By the map the dis-tance from Hekla to Duin da Ghaoith is some eighty-five miles, yet even at this great distance it could be seen that the twin tops of the hill were powdered with fresh snow. Curiously enough although Beinn Mor on Mull is 600ft higher than Duin da Ghaoith, the greater hill appeared free of snow to the top.

Bearing slightly more to the west one saw the long island of Coll – where a branch of the MacLeans of Duart held sway for centuries – and behind it the Ross, or western peninsula of Mull. West of that, again, was Tiree with its three hills – Ceann a'Bharra, Beinn Hynish, and Beinn Hough.

Almost directly behind Coll rose the Paps of Jura, plainly visible. Now from Hekla to the Jura tops just over 100 miles of sea, hill, and islands extend. It seemed almost unbelievable that hills of no great height – they average just under 2500ft – could be seen at so immense a distance, yet the Jura hills are unmistak-

* These exact measurements were solemnly vouched for!

able. But then, the exceptional clearness of the atmosphere may be judged from the fact that at least a dozen trawlers could be seen at work between Skerryvore and Barra, though the more outlying of those vessels must have been close on fifty miles away.

The Cuchulain Hills of Skye — named after that Ossianic hero commonly known as Cuchulain — seemed but a stone's throw distant, and away behind them were the snowcapped peaks of Knoydart on the mainland. About the entrance to Loch Bracadale the long swell could be seen breaking white. On the distant north-east horizon was a snowy hill which appeared to be An Teallach in Wester Ross. From the south face of this hill the sun had melted even,' particle of snow; its north slopes were of unbroken whiteness.

North-east, and far off, lay the Shiant, or Bespelled Islands, set far out into the Minch, where there dwelt, under enchantment, a grey seal of an unbelievable age. On the largest of the Shiant Isles was formerly a chapel, dedicated to the Virgin Mary.

Across the narrow arm of the sea north of Benbecula lay North Uist with its golden sands. Far out from those sands were the small group of uninhabited isles of Haskeir. Here more than anywhere the long Atlantic swell broke in white spray, with unhurried rhythm and majestic force. So inaccessible are these isles they may be impossible to reach for months on end, yet in bygone centuries monks had their home here, and the name of one of the islands — Haskeir Niamannich — signifies the Monks' Rock.

What an expanse of country one viewed this autumn day!

On the one hand, Mull, Skerryvore, Jura; on the other, St Kilda and the Flannan Isles. And stretching away for endless leagues the wide and windy plains of the Atlantic. Today these plains were of a wonderful and exceptional calmness. Scarce a ripple disturbed them. Everywhere the sky was clear, save in the far north-west, where St Kilda was from time to time hidden in rain. Over these ocean plains light and shade alternated. The waters were of many colours — opal, cobalt blue, amethystine, turquoise. Here and there a faint breeze of wind ruffled the waters, then died away. The trawlers as they fished seemed toy ships, so minute were they.

Gradually the sun sank westward. From afar, travelling from the north, appeared a gaggle of wild geese. Moving quickly and evenly south, and flying in one long line, they passed at a considerable distance below me. One conjectured what country was their goal. Was it Barra, or Islay perhaps, or had they in the mind's eye the Irish coast — Malahide with its abundance of feeding, or the windswept coasts of Donegal or Connemara?

Beneath Hekla lay the low country of South Uist with innumerable lochs, chief among them Loch Druidibeag and Loch Bee, both ramifying far into the brown moorlands.

So stormy had been the autumn, the hay and oats still remained in the fields.

About one's feet, as one sat at the hilltop, the minute alpine willow grew, its leaves golden with the coming of autumn. Plants of sea thrift were green as in midsummer, though without flowers.

Across the shoulder of the hill a peregrine falcon sped, the sun shining full upon his handsome plumage. Soon three ravens appeared, two of them sparring with beak and claws. From far below came the hoarse bark of a great black-backed gull.

As one reached Loch Druidibeag the sun had disappeared behind a dark cloud far over the Atlantic. The surface of the loch was so still that, even at a distance, one could discern the rings of a few rising trout.

An impetuous merlin crossed the loch in hot pursuit of a grey crow, following with supreme skill the swerves of the fugitive as it endeavoured to elude its opponent of swift flight.

Dusk fell swiftly, and in the still air was a touch of frost. But for long the last of the sunset lingered over the Atlantic, and when darkness had at length fallen, the flashing lamp from the lighthouse that is upon the Monach Islands stabbed the gloom with its white rays.

CHAPTER XVI
A Winter Climb: Beinn Mor Mull

MUILE NAM MOR BHEANN — or Mull of the Great Hills — has but one peak over 3000ft and that is Beinn Mor, or, in English, the Great Hill. One hears this name for an outstanding hill in many parts of the Highlands. Beinn Mor, or Beinn Mhor, is found upon South Uist, in Assynt in the northern Highlands, above Crianlarich in western Perthshire, and in many other districts as well.

Around Beinn Mor Mull many hills rise, but the highest of them is a good 600ft below the Big Hill.

Amongst these lesser tops are Beinn Buidhe, Beinn Fada, Beinn Bhearnach, Beinn Talaidh, Duin da Ghaoith.

Amongst all these hills deep glens lie with not a few lochs where trout and salmon have their home, and everywhere in the distance — gloomy or glistening, according to the day — are the tireless waters of the Atlantic.

The winter of which I write had been kind along the western seaboard, and even the highest hills had rarely been powdered with snow up to that December day on which I climbed Beinn Mor.

In the light of the pale winter sun the waters of the Sound of Mull sparkled this winter morning. About the rocks of Scallcastle many brown seals were lying, drowsy or fast asleep. They were of various colours and sizes, one of them almost as big as the grey Atlantic seal itself. But it is seldom that the true grey seal enters the Sound of Mull, or indeed any sheltered waters — its home is the open sea, where it rolls and tumbles through the long waves, undismayed during the fiercest storm.

On a large stone a pair of ringed plover slept; herons stood, motionless and silent, at their fishing, and widgeon fed amongst the bladder-wrack. A buzzard sailed high above the waters of the Sound, where a party of handsome oyster-catchers were dozing; the dark form of the buzzard did not arouse them. A great northern diver swam leisurely near, diving for its food. After a time the large bird came to the surface with a shellfish of some sort, which it had great difficulty in eating. The victim at length swallowed, this great diver — known to the Gael as Muir Bhuachaille, or the Herdsman of the Sea — called several times with low, far-carrying cry.

It would be interesting to know how arose this curious name, Sea Herdsman. What are the herds it tends far out in the open ocean? Are they the tribe of the grey seal, or the whales perhaps? The name may have been given this fine diver from the fact that the Gael believes it to be incapable of rising from the water — although this belief is quite erroneous, for the great northern diver can fly both fast and high, though it very seldom does so.

Along the shore of Loch nan Ceall the wind was strong and freshening. Squalls crossed the loch, as so often is the case when the wind is from the south-east; the air was hazy and the summit of Beinn Mor mist-capped. But the breeze was mild, and no speck of snow lay anywhere, even upon the highest ground. At a point just short of the Gribun rocks the road was left and the climb commenced. At first the gradient was easy. Small buttercups still blossomed on the hillside, though the grass was browned by the winter winds. Across the leaden sky drifted grey clouds, travelling with the speed of an express train, and one thought of the small mail steamer now midway between Mull and the distant Isle of Tiree, where, in a south-east gale, landing is impossible. But here, on the sheltered side of Beinn Mor, the air was still except for an occasional eddying gust. As one rose the clouds became darker; in the big corrie of Beinn Mor gloom and an inky darkness brooded. Lower and lower swept the mists; the sky to the northward was of a menacing green as though presaging a storm.

Along the ridge west of the big corrie the climb is an easy one. Even at 2500ft sheep were grazing and, curiously enough, the grass was greener by far than at sea level. But of bird life there was no sign — not even the feather of a ptarmigan.

There is a tradition that upon the south side of Beinn Mor is a spring holding an amber-coloured stone with curious properties. It is said that this stone can be left all day in the heart of a peat fire and yet remain as cold as when it was first taken from the well!

Above 2500ft grass is found but sparingly upon Beinn Mor. Basaltic 'scree', reminding one somewhat of the rough Spitsbergen hills, lies everywhere.
Just after midday the mist lessened. Gradually it rose until, save for a few hurrying wisps, the hilltop was clear and remained so for the rest of the day.

There is little level ground about the summit of Beinn Mor. South-west the hill slopes away sharply; north-east is an almost sheer precipice. The rushing of the wind as it swept across the dark rocks to windward made one realise the force of the gale, though upon the narrow ridge the air was almost still — for the uprushing current of wind passed high overhead.

About the hilltop grew plants of sea thrift, with a few saxifrages among them, now browned and withered by winter storms. The temperature was a single degree above freezing point, but the ground was quite without frost.

From the summit of Beinn Mor in clear weather an unsurpassed view is obtained, but today the south-east wind brought haze with it, as always.

Eastward, a cloud rested on Duin da Ghaoith, but Beinn Bhcarnach above Ardura was clear. Beside Ardura is a lochan, small and insignificant, but, so tradition has it, without bottom. It is narrated that when the Witch, or *Calliach* of Beinn Bhreac in the Lochaber country used to visit her Mull relative, known as the *Doiteag Mhuileach*, she often mentioned that when she crossed the hundred-fathom deep Sound of Mull the waters were not above her knees, whereas when fording the Cran Lochan (as the Ardura tarn is named) she was wet to the thigh!

Southward, directly below Beinn Mor, lay Glen Mor, or the Big Glen, which traverses Mull from one coastline to the other. How many associations and traditions has this little-known glen of the West! Many of them are lost, for the old *ceilidh*, or winter evening gathering, is now a thing of the past in Mull, and the younger generation have little interest in the old legends. It is said that, one evening long ago, two men were walking through Glen Mor. As they walked they boasted, one to the other, of the wonderful deeds they had done, of the yet more wonderful deeds they would do. Two hills overlooking the glen — Creach Bheinn and Beinn Buidhe — overheard this boastful talk. Said the mountains in loud and awful tones, which the affrighted travellers could not but overhear, 'Hark how these two little fellows boast; they must be given a lesson.'

Now in a pool of the Lussa, just at the bend of the stream above Torr an Eas, there dwelt a dreaded supernatural monster, the *tarbh uisge*, or water bull, who enticed wanderers to the black depths of his watery home. One of the men, shrewdly suspecting that the *tarbh uisge* would be put on their track by the two hills, loaded his gun with a 'charm', a silver sixpence. Sure enough, at the bend of the river stood the water bull awaiting his victims. But against the silver six-pence he was powerless, and was forced in humiliation to seek once more his retreat in the peaty pool.

The end of such a tale is not always so happy, and a small tarn in the forest land of Lochbuie takes its name — the Loch of the Maidens — from the fact that more than one lass, when out herding the cattle perhaps, was lured to the loch by a *tarbh uisge* and never heard of more.

Today, but a stone's throw (so it seemed) distant, the waters of Loch Schidain sparkled in the sunlight that had now displaced the mist. At the mouth of the loch is the hill known as Bearraich, from which, on a clear day of May, I have seen the whole of the north Irish coast, faint and ethereal, on the southern horizon.

Towards afternoon the misty haze cleared somewhat, and out to sea showed the small Isle of Staffa, with the long Atlantic swell breaking white about its caves. Beyond it, and scarce visible, lay the Dutchman's Cap and the long grassy isle of Lunga where puffins and guillemots make their summer home and shearwaters skim of a June evening. Nearer at hand were Eorsa, that lion-shaped island set in the centre of Loch nan Ceall, and the greater isles of Ulva and Gometra, extend-ing westward into the Atlantic.

When first I had arrived upon the hilltop all the great hills of the mainland had been hidden in mist and haze, but gradually they showed themselves. Emerging above the dark haze that hid Oban and the lesser hills of Lorne, the twin tops of Beinn Cruachan stood as though suspended in mid-air. Bearing northward were the faint outlines of other hills — Ben Starav, Beinn Sguliard, Bidean nam Beann, Ben Nevis itself. On none of these hills, so far as could be seen, did any snow lie.

Fighting the gale, and exulting in their power, a pair of peregrine falcons crossed the hilltop where I sat. Moving aslant the wind they sped, the falcon, as they passed, markedly larger than the male or tiercel. The falcon flew within a stone's throw; the tiercel, being lighter, was caught on the up-rushing current and lifted high above me. With what consummate skill did the hen bird make use of the gale! Her wings were bent back so far that they seemed almost pressed against her sides — in the position she would assume when 'stooping' on her prey.

Soon both she and her mate passed from view, and for the space of a few minutes the hilltop was deserted. Then, at precisely the same point at which the peregrines first appeared, a pair of golden eagles came in sight. Far larger and heavier birds than the peregrine, the eagles seemed to feel the force of the wind less, and, rising easily on the swift air current, soared high above the hilltop for a space before moving eastward in the teeth of the storm.

With the dusk the gale increased in force. Upon Loch nan Ceall fierce squalls were raising the waters in clouds of white spray; the piping of ringed plover and oystercatchers mingled with the rush of the wind.

Soon darkness hid each loch and hill, and the sea, too, was invisible save where the lights of a sheltering trawler shone brightly through the gloom.

CHAPTER XVII
Winter on Beinn Cruachan

FROM THAT deep and hill-girt arm of the sea, Loch Etive, rises abruptly Beinn Cruachan, or the Hill of the Many Peaks. After much mild and unsettled weather along the Atlantic seaboard, during which rain fell almost constantly aslant the humid south-west wind, mid-January brought two superb days to the West, and on the second of these days my wife and I made the ascent of the hill.

Beinn Cruachan, one of the highest hills of Argyllshire, reaches a height of 3689ft above sea level. It is so precipitous that the snow never lies upon its western face to any great depth. During a day of strong wind I have seen the snow lifted up from the higher slopes of the hill at least a couple of hundred feet above the top.

But this morning as we left Taynuilt the air was breathless, and a keen frost was binding the ground. A three-mile walk brought us to the Bridge of Awe, and the base of the hill. Gradually the light became stronger, for the mornings are late in breaking in January in the West. The conical summit of the beinn stood out against the cloudless sky with great distinctness, its snows in the half-light seeming of a greenish-grey. At length the sun, striking on the south-east side of the cone, transformed the snow to crimson. But to the valley of the Awe the beams could not penetrate, for the encircling hills were too steep for the low winter sun to surmount.

The River Awe ran swift and full, hurrying to the waters of Loch Etive.

The distance from the river bank to the summit of Cruachan is not far, but the climb is extremely steep. Today the low slopes of the hill, above which gulls soared and kestrels hovered, were covered with a sprinkling of snow, just sufficient on the steep gradient to make each step a thing of uncertainty and progress painfully slow. At length the hills of the Isle of Mull, far to the west of us, showed themselves, their covering of snow extending almost to sea level. Beneath them, so it seemed, lay the fertile Isle of Lismore.

At 1000ft above sea level snow lay on Beinn Cruachan to the depth of three or four inches. Beneath us there flew leisurely a great black-backed gull, its course high above the River Awe. From the hilltop a peregrine falcon volplaned at great speed.

Over the whole of the mountain intense stillness brooded. Not a croak of a ptarmigan, not a cry of a grouse, broke that stillness. Indeed, during the whole of the day, we neither saw nor heard a single ptarmigan. To one who is familiar with the Cairngorm Hills in central Scotland, this absence of ptarmigan is striking, for we passed a sun-bathed corrie, apparently well-suited to these mountain dwellers, yet no tracks of them did we see. At 2000ft the frost was intense. Each spring was frozen, and the hidden ice, beneath nearly half a foot of powdery snow, made walking precarious. At 3000ft we stood on the summit of one of the spurs of Cruachan — by name, Meall Cuanail.

Not a breath of air stirred here. The sun shone with almost summer warmth. South-west Loch Awe lay. On its quiet surface, which stretched away almost to the horizon, a minute steamboat threaded its way, brown smoke pouring from its funnel.

Now the view westward had opened out — hill, glen and sea, all bathed in soft winter sunlight. Every hill on Mull was distinct. Rising steeply from the Sound of Mull was Duin da Ghaoith. At its base stood the Castle of Duart, the home for centuries of the chiefs of the MacLeans, who formerly held great possessions in this West country.

A few miles nearer to us, showing white and needle-like against the waters of the Firth of Lorne, was the lighthouse of Lismore, situated in that part of the Firth where many swift currents meet. Beinn Mor, the highest of the Mull hills, was — an uncommon thing in winter — mist-free and bathed in sunshine to the summit, its precipitous slopes glistening white. Against the rocks at the entrance to Lochbuie, where formerly the eagle nested, and where wild goats still climb about the great precipices, the long Atlantic swell broke lazily. South-west, as far as the eye could reach, stretched the plains of the Atlantic. For a few miles off-shore a slight breeze ruffled the waters, beyond this all was stillness. A rare day this, in mid-winter, when Nature was altogether at rest, even away from the shelter of the most outlying headland. The Ross of Mull was invisible, for the high ground above Lochbuie hid all beyond it. Nor could the distant Outer Hebrides be discerned. But on the western horizon lay the low shape of the Isle of Colonsay, the former home of the MacNeills of that ilk.

The last 600ft of Beinn Cruachan were, this cloudless day of January, the hardest part of the climb.

Snow lay thick on the ground, and the crevices between the boulders, with which the upper slopes of the hill are covered, were treacherously hidden. Even at a height of 3500ft very little old snow lay on the ground — only a few isolated drifts. The covering had fallen the previous night, when a sharp, though short-lived snowstorm had visited western Argyll.

In the powdery snow were the tracks of fox and mountain hare. One of these hares we disturbed almost at the very summit of the hill, its coat as white as the surrounding snow. The mountain hare is smaller than its relative of the low country, and a golden eagle is able to lift it, screaming, aloft, without apparent effort.

Each boulder today was thickly encrusted with delicate fog crystals — feathery spikelets projecting against the moisture-laden wind that swept the hilltop at the time when they were formed. Many of them were wonderfully beautiful, resembling miniature oak leaves. These fog crystals are confined for the most part to the high tops, where fog or mist is present almost continuously during the winter months.

The west top of Cruachan (3611ft above the sea) was reached two hours after midday. The cairn was deeply encrusted with snow and ice, and upwards of eight inches of snow covered the hilltop. The air was still; even at this height the sun shone warmly.

North, south and east stood hill upon hill, deeply snow-clad and coldly grand against the cloudless winter sky.

Almost directly beneath the hilltop — so abrupt was the slope — Loch Etive lay. The original Gaelic name of this loch is said to have been Loch Eitidh, or the Stormy Loch, from the heavy squalls that sweep so suddenly down upon it from the high hills. But today only the lightest of northerly breezes ruffled its blue surface. Steaming from Bon Awe, and steering towards the tidal race known as the Falls of Lora (*Luath Sruth* — Quick Current) and the open sea beyond, was a steamer which at this great height seemed a toy ship. At the head of the loch there rose steeply the imposing bulk of Beinn Starav (3541ft). So clear was Ben Nevis, thirty miles distant, that the snow-covered ruins of the observatory on the hilltop were distinct. Upon the north-western horizon the peaks of Knoydart were clear. Atlantic sentinels, they look out over the restless waters of the Minch on to the Cuchulain Hills of Skye. Nearer at hand, but still across the waters of distant Loch Linnhe, or the Loch of Striving, as an old Gaelic name has it, one could see Beinn Hiant, or the Bespelled Hill of Ardnamurchan, Scotland's most western mainland promontory. Beyond it, and standing between the little port of Mallaig and the chain of the Outer Hebrides, were the snow-powdered peaks of the Isle of Rhum.

So clear was the air that the small mailboat could be seen leaving the port of Craignure, in the Isle of Mull, and setting her course for Loch Aline (or the Beautiful Loch) in Morvern opposite. South-west rose the hills of Jura, and beyond them Islay and its heights. Beyond Loch Awe a portion of Loch Fyne was visible, and behind it again the Kyles of Bute and the Arran hills. Nearer at hand rose the mountainous island of Scarba, and the Garvellach Islands, or Isles of the Sea, as they are sometimes called, set at the entrance to the Firth of Lorne. South and east Ben Lomond, Ben Ime, Ben Lui — to name only a few — were distinct on the horizon, and beyond Ben Lomond a great cloud hung, perhaps the smoke of Glasgow. North-east rose the splendid hills of the Black Mount Forest.

Such is a faint outline of the prospect, this January day, when the sun shone with unusual warmth so that the icicles upon the rocks were thawed and the snow became soft and sticky.

The sun was dipping towards the south-west horizon as we left the cairn. A few lines of cirrus clouds, at an immense height, were now appearing on the Atlantic horizon, and through them the sun shone with soft light. Near the cairn were the tracks of a fox, a spot of blood upon the virgin whiteness of the snow showing where reynard had rested a moment while carrying his prey to his lair.

The sun was setting as we reached the lower ground. Beinn Starav in its glow took on a salmon-pink colour, and upon Cruachan itself the snowy boulders were crimsoned. And then the sun, shortly after four o'clock, disappeared from even the highest tops, and the pale moon in her first quarter gradually gathered strength, and, with Venus shining brightly beside her, shed her beams upon a snow-clad world while the frost bound still firmer the earth.

CHAPTER XVIII
The Serpent of Glen Mor:
A Tradition of the Isle of Mull

ACROSS MULL a lonely glen leads. Its name is Glen Mor, and it is, as often as not, a place of hurrying mists, and rain that sweeps across from the south-west in incredible downpours.

But there are days in winter — though they have been all too rare of recent years — when the gales are stilled, when the skies are clear, and when the hills and the glen itself are deep in a dazzling covering of snow.

It is a wild and unfrequented glen, and treeless save for a wood of stunted oak and birch known as *Doire na Chulain*, beside the Lussa. To the wanderer traversing Glen Mor from Ardura upon Loch Spelve it is a lonely place, even for Mull.

There are but two houses between the tidemark and the watershed, just under 700ft above the Atlantic. One of the dwellings is a shepherd's cottage. Torr an Eas, it is called, and stands just above the *Eas* or waterfall of the Lussa where the small river drops foaming, after a time of rain, into a deep yeasty pool beloved of the race of salmon and sea trout.

In this cottage lives — or lived — a charming old lady who had no word of English, but who always offered a welcome and generous hospitality; creamy milk, fresh from the cow, crisp oatcakes, scones of enormous proportions. Her son, the shepherd, was usually abroad upon the hill.

The other habitation is a larger one, but also the home of a shepherd. It is two miles farther into Glen Mor, where the Lussa broadens out into a number of hill lochs, and its name is Inshriff, a corruption, perhaps, of some Gaelic word. These are the only two houses until the watershed is passed, and one commences the descent to Loch Scridain.

On the western slope of Glen Mor are likewise but a couple of houses — a small croft at Craig and a stalker's house at Ulvalt so that the glen throughout the whole of its dozen miles from shore to shore is a very lonely one.

Opposite Inshriff, but rather farther down the glen, on the slope of Beinn Fhada (pronounced Ben Add) is a longish knoll. It stands above the River Lussa, and is known as Cnoc Fada, or the Long Knowe. It may be nearly 200 yards in length, with one side very steep and perhaps 30ft high, with a curious serpent-shaped bend upon it. Here, long ago, was the dwelling-place of a great and fearsome serpent or *beithir*. Now this Gaelic word — of which the English sound is 'bear' — signifies no ordinary serpent, but refers to a monster of the dragon type, but without wings. One sees the name in Beinn Bheithir, that lofty hill rising steeply from Ballachulish near Glen Goe, and the *beithir* of that hill and Glen Mor may be one and the same monster.

Now, even in the days of the serpent, tradition has it that a track led through Glen Mor, and the dragon with its lair on Cnoc Fada lay constantly on the watch for man or beast who should be so bold as to journey through the glen. The old track through Glen Mor passed nearer to the serpent's hiding-place than the present road, and, so cunning and insatiable was the dragon, no living creature escaped it. The glen became deserted, a place dreaded by all.

At length, to such a pass did matters come, a messenger was sent to the king. A great reward was now offered by the Crown for the destruction of the dragon, and a ship with its crew was placed at the disposal of any man daring enough to make the attempt. So dreadful was the dragon, and so far and wide had its powers been noised abroad, it was long before any man was found who ventured to pit himself against the slayer of man and beast. But at length such a one came forward and with the ship assigned to him entered the blue waters of Loch Scridain, anchoring his vessel near the middle of the loch.

No doubt as he passed the saintly Isle of Iona that guards Loch Scridain and the Ross of Mull from the fury of the Atlantic he offered up to Saint Columba a prayer that his perilous venture might be crowned with success. Having anchored his ship, he at once set about preparing his plan for the destruction of the *beithir*, and a very skilled and unusual one it was, too. Between the ship and the shore a strong cable was stretched, having a number of casks attached to it at intervals. Each of the casks, and the cable itself, were spiked with sharp iron points, facing every direction. When the last barrel had been spiked the bold fellow landed from his ship upon the shore of Loch Scridain, taking a number of horses with him. These he tethered at intervals along the road leading toward Glen Mor and the dreaded Cnoc Fada. Mounting now upon his remaining steed he approached the dragon's lair. The *beithir*, even while yet he was some distance away, scented him out and, rearing itself on end, gave chase horribly.

Now began a desperate pursuit. Horse and rider were being overtaken quickly when the first relay was reached. Leaping upon the fresh steed the man fled forward once more, the serpent momentarily lagging behind to crunch the bones of the abandoned horse. Each fresh mount was just sufficient to carry the man to where the next was awaiting him, and each wretched animal was in turn swallowed by the dragon — which from all accounts must have been having the feed of its life!

But at last Loch Scridain was in view; at last its welcome shore was gained. A boat, manned by a sturdy crew, anxiously awaited the flying horseman. Leaping from his exhausted steed the adventurer, as he was rowed quickly out to his vessel, saw the tireless and still ravenous dragon devouring his last horse.

Now must have ensued some anxious moments, for the success or failure of he whole plan was to be tested.

The dragon, seeing its enemy escaping to his ship, entered the loch. But it was helpless in the water, and there remained to it but one way in which it could reach the ship, and that was across the cable with its spiked barrels. Crawling unsteadily upon the cable the fearsome apparition approached the ship. Those on board watched it, fascinated. Scarce daring to breathe, they realised that they, and even the ship herself, would have no chance against so terrible an adversary. Their one hope lay in the carefully prepared spikes, and sure enough the monster soon became in difficulties. Its strength was of no avail except upon the earth, and gradually its coils became entangled amongst the spikes. Desperately it endeavoured to free itself. From innumerable wounds its blood dripped, so that the waters of Loch Scridain were stained for miles around. At length it became exhausted, so that the ship's crew once more took to their small boat and with little difficulty administered the *coup de grâce*.

Thus was Glen Mor delivered of its evil monster, and now man and beast may pass through the glen without fear. Indeed there are very few persons alive today who know the old legend. But when the winter's wind rushes from the storm-tossed Atlantic across Glen Mor, and when upon Beinn Bhuidhe and Beinn Mor the drifting snows are hurried on the arms of the gale; when from the lochs the water is caught up in spindrift, and on the rocky slopes of Beinn Bhearnach the mountain hares and ptarmigan crouch in sheltered hollows, then, perhaps, as some of the old people toil painfully through the glen, with the gathering night upon them and with squalls of hail and quick-travelling winter thunder overhead, they involuntarily give a thought to the dreaded *beithir*, and nervously speed their steps as they pass by the little knoll on Beinn Fhada where in far-off times so many tragedies were enacted.

CHAPTER XIX
The Island Piper

WESTWARD OF Lorne is Mull, and westward of that, again, is the rocky Isle of Coll. It is a long island, and viewed from the seas around it appears a place of dreariness and desolation, but this first impression is deceptive, for there is fertile land in plenty in the interior of the island.

Yet there are few of the old native crofters now upon the isle, for during recent years strangers from the south, both farmers and tradespeople, have settled here.

The island was always of peculiar interest to me, because of the fact that an old piper had his home upon it. He was well past four score years, yet his vigour was remarkable, and his intellect – he had an unusually fine one – as keen as ever up to his last illness. I have never met a crofter with so wide a knowledge of West Highland affairs, and his breadth of view and his inexhaustible store of reminiscences would have been noteworthy in any man, whatever his station in life. But it was chiefly as a piper that he attracted me, for it was refreshing to find one who knew the old tunes, and could talk intimately of past masters of the *piob mhor* long since dead.

The old piper's croft stood on the western side of the island. Within a stone's throw of the door the long Atlantic waves broke with a deep, soothing sound upon a strip of golden sand. On the horizon, as often as not, one could see the herring drifters rise and fall upon the swell that is rarely absent from the Coll banks. It was a peaceful spot, and of a clear summer's night the westering sun bathed all the long chain of the Outer Hebrides, and shone ruddy on the conical heights of Rhum and of the Skye hills behind them.

Although the old piper was still vigorous and his fingers retained their cunning, it was never easy to persuade him to take down his ancient chanter from the shelf. He had little patience with the young players round him, for they contented themselves with the music of march, strathspey and reel, which the veteran considered immeasurably inferior to the *Ceol Mor*, or Big Music, which he played so well in his younger days. The aged piper was positive that the old masters – the great players of bygone centuries – never demeaned themselves by playing marches and reels – 'tinkers' music', as the old man sweepingly called it. Indeed, according to him, they were never permitted to do so, and the Chieftain of Coll nearly dismissed one of the best pipers he ever had when, returning unexpectedly to his castle at Breachachadh, he heard that piper (thinking his master well out of earshot) playing a march for his own gratification.

Except among pipers, there is now much ignorance, even amongst Highlanders, of the different types of pipe music. The *Ceol Mor*, or Big Music, is very old; is usually, though not always, played slowly, and is the true or classical music of the big Highland pipe. To this class of pipe music there belong the cumha, or lament; the *failte*, or salute; and the more animated *caismeachd*, or war song. To compare these tunes with a strathspey or reel is like comparing a master-piece by Chopin with the latest air that all the town is humming – tuneful and delightful, perhaps, but not to be contrasted with a piece of classical music. Yet there are many who fail to distinguish between a *piobaireachd* (as the Big Music is sometimes called) and march, strathspey and reel.

Only last year, at a well-known Highland meeting, I was asked by an acquaintance who, with apparent understanding, was listening to the piping of an expert, 'Is that a *piobaireachd* or a march?' Now it happened that a particularly lively march was being played at the time, and so the query came as something of a shock – and not so much because of the ignorance displayed (that, unfortunately, is all too common) as because it was shown by a person who appeared to appreciate pipe music.

But the old piper upon sea-girt Coll was for many years before his death too frail to make the long sea passage to Oban, so he knew little of how the world of pipers fared – his mind was in the past. He had received his piping lessons more than sixty years ago from an uncle in Canada, who in turn had been instructed by a Coll piper who had received his tuition from the last of the MacCrimmons – Donald Ruadh by name– the celebrated hereditary pipers of the chiefs of the MacLeods for generations.

To the piping school of the MacCrimmons at Boreraig, in the shadow of the old castle of Dunvegan, there came in olden days pipers from all parts of the Scottish Highlands, and even from Ireland. What the standard of playing was in that far-off time we have no means of knowing, yet it must have been a high one, for it was said that the MacCrimmons counted no pupil proficient in less than seven years.

It was all *piobaireachd* or Big Music that was played in those days in the Dunvegan school of piping, and thus it was only natural that the old piper of Coll should have considered that class of pipe music as the only thing worth playing. It was, as I have said, no easy matter to persuade him to play, but of a December's evening, when the wind moaned without and when the peat fire burned brightly in the small room, the veteran's interest in far-off days would be roused by the notes of his chanter. At first he would play haltingly, as though his old fingers were finding it no easy task to express the music that ran in his head. But as he warmed to his task his mind would wander back to the time of his youth, and, with tightly shut eyes, he would play through one *piobaireachd* after another. They were very old tunes, such as *A'Ghlas Mheur* (The Finger Lock), *Cruinneachadh Chloinn Chatain* (The Gathering of Clan Chattan), *Ruaig Ghlinn Freoine* (The Rout of Glen Fruin), *Failte Phrionnsa* (The Prince's Salute), *Maol Donn*, a Uist *piobaireachd*, composed — so the old piper believed — on the grief of a widow when her cow was lost on the moorland bogs, and many others. One of his favourites was that most sad and solemn *piobaireachd*, The Lament for the Only Son, or in Gaelic *Cumha an Aona Mhic*, and he told me that the old pipers played that tune always on the occasions of greatest grief.

One stirring tune the piper loved to play. It was, he said, performed in the old times by the pipers of two opposing clans, and was known as *Brosnachadh Catha*. As the clansmen engaged in the most fierce and desperate conflict their pipers stood a little to one side and played this tune, sometimes known as 'The Stimulus'. Faster and faster, more wildly and yet more wildly, they urged on their clansmen to the best of their ability.

The tune was said to have been played for the first time in 1396, in the reign of King Robert III at the Battle of the North Inch at Perth. In this fight thirty of the Clan Chattan contended with an equal number of the 'Clankay' — who, some say, were the Davidsons, and others the Clan Cameron — in mortal combat. The fight was to be commenced at the sound of a horn, and a great crowd (human life was of little account in those far-off days) assembled to see it.

At the last moment the Chief of the Clan Chattan — Shaw of Rothiemurchus — found he had only twenty-nine men (the thirtieth had probably fled), so he went across to the crowd and asked if any of them would fight in the place of his absent follower. A certain blacksmith agreed to join him, and it was largely through the prowess of the smith that all save one of the opposing clan were either killed or wounded. The Chamberlain Rolls of 1396-7 have, I am informed by a direct descendant of that Shaw of Rothiemurchus, an interesting entry of £14 2s. 1d. for timber, iron, and the erection of the 'lists' for the sixty persons fighting on the Inch.

During the fight a piper from both the clans stood aside and played *Brosnachadh Catha*.

In those days the Highland pipe had but two drones; the big drone was not added until the latter part of the fifteenth or beginning of the sixteenth century. Yet the music can have differed little from that which today has so inspiring an effect upon Scotsmen the world over.

There were tunes and 'tunings' (in the days of the MacCrimmons certain 'tunings', or short pieces of music, were played by the great pipers when getting their pipes into trim), which the veteran piper feared would be lost at his death, and his delight when I mastered such a tune was charming to see. 'That's it, that's it; now you have it,' he would say, jumping up from his chair excitedly, and then he would set to and play the old air once again, lingering lovingly upon the notes. It was good to see his pleasure, yet it was not easy to follow his playing, for he hurried somewhat, and, as he had no knowledge of staff notation, was unable to set the notes on paper. 'Ah,' he used to say, 'there is no person now that takes an interest in the old tunes.' How could he, living upon his remote isle, know that the 'old tunes' were being played — and played very well, too? He felt that the ancient spirit of piping had been lost by present-day players; yet in this idea he was probably wrong, but in old age one often may be dogmatic.

His information concerning the old tunes of the bagpipe he was ever ready and glad to give. For a man of his great age his handwriting was marvellously clear. Each letter was a work of art, each word well-chosen, each page packed full of interesting information; so that his writings were always a delight to receive, and it was at times difficult to realise they were the productions of a Hebridean crofter.

He had much to say of the MacArthurs, the hereditary pipers of the MacQuaries of Ulva, who formerly had their college on Ulva Island (he himself had heard the last of the MacArthurs play), of the MacKays, the hereditary pipers of the MacKenzies of Gairloch, and of not a few others. And the point he repeatedly emphasised was that the playing of all those master hands was so similar and so faultless that it was impossible, almost, to tell who was performing, unless the piper was actually seen. According to him, when playing a *piobaireachd*, the performer, during the 'theme' or *urlar* marched in time with the tune, slowly, according to the nature of the composition. At each 'variation' or *siubhal*, and its doubling and trebling (if these were present) he stood still, placing the right foot foremost at the first part of the variation, and the left at the latter part. In like manner he stood during the playing of the *Taorluadh* and the *Crunluadh* of the tune, and did not march as do present-day pipers.

Living on Coll, an island so long in the possession of the MacLeans of Coll, it was only natural that the old piper should have much to say regarding those chieftains and the *piobaireachdan* which pertained more especially to them. The Rankines were the hereditary' pipers of the MacLeans of Duart in Mull. MacLean of Coll, on a visit to Duart his chief, took one of the Rankines (Neil by name) from Duart to Coll. Thus, my old friend maintained, the celebrated Dr Johnson as in error when, on a visit to Coll, he wrote that the Rankines were hereditary pipers of the MacLeans of Coll.

But perhaps we may excuse the learned doctor, as a Southerner, his little inexactitude!

Well, the old piper has gone now, and there is none on Coll, or on Tiree either, to perpetuate the old compositions he loved so well. His tunes have died with him, for some of those he played are never heard at the present day.

There are those who hold that his piping was incorrect, but then the playing of *piobaireachd* is ever a controversial subject among pipers, and it is scarcely fair to be too dogmatic concerning music, the newest compositions of which are at least 100 years old; the finest forms having been composed 300 to 400 years ago.

It is conceded the MacCrimmons were peerless as pipers, yet each school of piping at the present day asserts that its own rendering of the tune is the MacCrimmons' rendering. hey cannot all be right, and it may be that theMacCrimmons' playing of the great tunes they composed is an art which they have carried with them to that spiritual realm beyond the western horizon of the Atlantic — *Rioghachd Fo Thuinn*, or the Realm Beneath the Waves.

CHAPTER XX
The Life of a Hebridean Crofter of South Uist

IT IS April, and the winter storms are past. Once more the sun shines out brightly upon the islands of the Hebrides – Barra, Eriskay and South Uist, Benbecula, North Uist and Lewis.

But in the strength of the spring sun the bareness of the land is but emphasised, for there is as yet no blade of green grass, even on the sheltered banks – all the country from the tidemark to the highest hill lies lifeless, or at all events asleep, after its winter struggle with the winds.

As the Canadian Pacific liner *Marloch* lay off Lochboisdale awaiting 300 emigrants for Alberta, a lady passenger on board exclaimed: 'How they will miss the sea!' This set me thinking. Yes, surely they will miss the sea in their new inland home, for their lives have been lived within sight and sound of the restless Atlantic, but it seemed to me that they would miss the wind fully as much.

No-one who has not lived upon the Hebrides can realise the important part the wind plays in the lives of the people. It is with them, in winter, constantly. It may blow for weeks with the force of half a gale with never a lull. Suddenly it may increase to hurricane force, as it did in March, 1921, when every second house in all the Hebrides was unroofed, and the inmates had to leave their dwellings which momentarily threatened to collapse! On that occasion the Northern Lighthouse Commissioner's steamer *Hesperus* was at anchor in the landlocked harbour of Castlebay, Barra Island, and even with both her anchors down was obliged to steam half speed ahead to escape being drifted on to the rocks!

Even in May the south-west and west wind may sweep across the Hebrides day and night, without a pause, averaging a speed of 20mph.

So in their new homes in Canada the Hebridean crofters will miss the sea and the wind, though they still will have the hills.

The crofter of the Isles has a hard life. It is one constant struggle against the forces of the elements, and all accounts seem to show that the seasons are changing for the worse.

No longer do frost and snow visit the islands in winter. Some of the old people can remember when the wild swans were frozen to death upon the lochs; now years may pass with no film of ice forming upon even the smallest of these lochs. And yet the cold winters of former years were more healthy and seasonable than those of present times. The winter now consists of one almost continuous storm of wind and rain, and I was told that during the past season of winter – 1922-3 – the thousand-foot hill of Heaval on Barra was sprinkled with white on one single occasion only. With the snow and frost of former times there came dryness; with the mild south-west wind of recent winters, moisture from the Atlantic flows across the land, so that the old people lie abed with rheumatism and even the younger generation feel their joints stiff and aching. And there is no protection against the wind, from whatever quarter it may blow, for almost all the crofting settlements are on the western seaboard of the isles, where the land is level and more fertile than in the slightly sheltered glens and hillsides of the eastern districts. Thus it easily may be imagined how eagerly the people of the Hebrides look forward to the passing of winter and the coming of the spring sun, and of 'steady weather', as they say.

One of the first signs that the departure of winter is imminent is the appearance of the yellow flower of St Brighid or Bride. This is the dandelion, and appears in sheltered ditches, on the south-facing thatched walls of the crofts, in the shelter of the stack yard, before February is out.

Then hope arises in the hearts of the old people, and they look forward eagerly to the lengthening day.

Their houses are small; there are no trees to shelter them; even a garden is a very rare thing. It must be a long and weary winter in these wee houses. The whole family eats and lives in a single small room. The floor is of earth, sprinkled with fine sand from the shore. Upon the hearth a peat fire burns. It is never permitted to die out and, when the family retires for the night, is kept alight by thrusting a wet peat into the embers and covering it over with them. There may be no chimney in the room; in that case the smoke escapes with difficulty through small slits between the walls and the roof, and the room is so filled with peat reek that it is not easy to see the inmates, while the eyes of the stranger smart and burn uncomfortably.

Even at midsummer these rooms are dark, for the windows are minute; it is through the open door that most of the daylight enters, and whenever the weather permits the door remains open. The doors of the houses are on the east or north-east side, in order to be sheltered as far as possible from the prevalent south-west winds. The single window, too, faces the same way.

The house is shared by the ducks and poultry, and a handloom may take up a good part of the living-room. The furnishing is simple – a wooden bench with dresser and table and one or two hard chairs completing the outfit.

In many ways these island dwellings call to mind the houses one sees along the west coast of Ireland, but there is one notable difference – in Ireland the pig is an important individual in every family; in the Hebrides it is unknown, or almost so. In Ireland the cattle are often under the same roof as the crofters, but in the Hebrides they are housed in beehive dwellings with no windows – separate from the living house and sometimes a little distance from it.

The long winter evenings must now seem even more wearisome than formerly, for in the old days there were *ceilidh*, or winter gatherings round the peat fire, at which many stories were told and many traditions were handed down from one generation to the next. But now the younger people have not the same interest in the old things; folklore and tales of the past do not appeal to them, and the *ceilidh* as an institution is dying out.

But there is much weaving still to be done of a winter's night, and much spinning of wool and knitting to keep the women busy. Not many years ago handwoven and natural dyed tartan was made in the Hebrides. Now the art has almost died out; the weavers of tartan can be counted on the fingers of one hand.

One might imagine that under such conditions the people of the Hebrides would go early to bed, yet one sees the lights in the small windows up to the 'wee smaa' hours', and it is after seven o'clock in the morning before many persons are astir. Even in summer some of the shops do not open until midday, and should one attempt to make a purchase at the incredibly early hour of 10am one learns that the storekeeper is still abed. On the other hand, it was frequently the hour of midnight before the merchant's delivery van reached the lodge where we have more than once stayed, and even at that late hour the driver had still to cover a distance of sixteen miles to his base for the night!

Let us follow the life of a Hebridean crofter from the time when the early April sunshine warms the thin soil and dries partially the sodden and mist-drenched moorlands.

There is little to be done on the land during April. The peaty earth is still too rain-soaked to be tilled, and the weather, even in May, is often so inclement that in the opinion of the islanders early sowing does not pay.

In the beginning of May the land is ploughed and the first of the 'barr dearg' or May-weed, gathered on the seashore.

This harvest is of the fronds of the seaweed known as *laminaria*, and when gathered at the tide is taken in carts to the level machair to dry, being afterwards burnt and sold as kelp ash, which yields potash and iodine.

May is a busy month in the Hebrides. The most important event – apart from the sowing of the crop – is the digging of the peats for the coming winter. Coal in the Outer Hebrides is almost unknown, and each small cottage has its peat stack, carefully built, which provides the inmates with warmth, and perhaps light as well, for a twelvemonth.

The peat moss is often miles away from the crofting community. If it be near a road the peats when dry are carted to the houses; if it be out on the moor they are carried in creels by the crofters – the women are as proficient as the men in this hard work – to the nearest road or track where a horse and cart may venture.

In Barra the ponies carry the peats on panniers across the moss to the nearest road— provided the ground is not too boggy for them to walk over.

I remember, one rainy day late in May, watching a number of men cutting their peats close beside the only plantation of trees — stunted veterans not above a dozen feet in height — on South Uist. It had been an unusually cold and dreary spring, and summer seemed as far off as ever. Suddenly, from the small assembly of storm-scarred trees, many of them uprooted and growing feebly where they lay, came the soft liquid notes of the cuckoo. Now in Uist the cuckoo, or 'enchanted bird' as it is sometimes called in Gaelic, is rare, and its stay upon the island is, at best, a fleeting one. It was interesting, therefore, to see each man stop abruptly in his digging as the aerial chimes of the cuckoo carried far across that rain-sodden Hebridean moor.

Although some of the best peat mosses of the Hebrides have been exhausted there is no danger of peat ever becoming scarce, for everywhere in the Outer Hebrides great stretches of bog land abound, and on much of it sphagnum moss grows. This moss is gradually dying, and as new plants take root upon the remains of the old the latter are pressed down and in the course of centuries are squeezed into an almost solid dark brown substance — peat. But peat varies considerably both in its colour and in its burning qualities. The best peat is probably thousands of years old. It is black and when dried is almost as hard as coal. The ash of this peat is white.

Not every peat moss produces these black peats; more frequently they are brown, comparatively soft, and easily broken. They burn more readily than those of harder texture, yet there is not the same 'body' in them, and their heat lasts only a short time. Their ash is brown or red brown. The digging of the peat, or *foid* as it is known in Gaelic, is done by a special spade (sometimes wooden) which slices off the spongy mass in slabs of the correct proportions. Usually one man slices off the peats while his companion catches them as they drop and lays them flat on the heather for the first stage of their drying. A skilled man may cut as many as 5000 peats in a single day.

When half dry the turfs are set up in threes — two on end, the third lying horizontally upon the other two — and when thoroughly dry are collected and stacked, usually in July.

In May the rye, barley, and oats are sown. Some of the poorer crofters have no horse or pony, and they must harrow their crops in themselves. I have watched an old woman drag laboriously a heavy harrow across her small field of new-sown oats during the last days of May, and have wondered how the crop could possibly come to maturity before the arrival of the winter storms. A few days before I had seen the crofter and his wife sow another part of the field, and then manure it by hand. The horse dung was carried in a pail, and was scattered over the newly sown oats as seed might have been. The earth was wet and sour; even at the best little return could be hoped for, and as likely as not the crop would be harvested sodden and half green at the end of October. The difficulties of seed time are such that I have seen old people sowing their small field on Uist as late as the first week of June – when the oats of the mainland were already well-braided.

Much of the Hebridean land is sour and peaty, but much of it along the western seaboard is almost pure sand. In fine weather this sand becomes warmed by the sun, so that the crops grow at a surprising rate, and no season is too wet for them, for the sandy soil soaks up the rain like a sponge.

As the young grass becomes green on the small fields the horses, cows and calves are tethered to a strong stake which is moved periodically from one part of the field to another as each narrow area becomes close-cropped – for there is no fence between the fields, and it is a common thing to see a calf or pony, which has broken loose, playing havoc with the young oats and barley. During the month of June there is still a certain amount of peat cutting to be done, but the chief work of the people now consists of drying and burning the seaweed for kelp.

On some of the Hebrides there is the fishing of lobsters during this month, but, apart from flounder-fishing in the Sound of Barra, there is little fishing upon South Uist, for there is no single harbour along the western side of the island. Thus the fishing is confined to a few families, and the island, through no fault of its own, loses annually a great harvest of the sea.

One often observes, these long June days, a woman making her way wearily from the white shore, across the green machair, to her croft perhaps a couple of miles distant from the tide. On her back she carries a large sack of fine sand for the earthen floor of her house. The better type of Hebridean crofter is a cleanly person, and takes a pride in keeping her wee house spotless.

In July weeds grow apace, so there is much work in hoeing the young potato crop. Sometimes each weed is uprooted by hand; a slow and tiring process, but one that is more thorough than trusting to the hoe. These early July days the machair is at its best. The grass at last grows vigorously, and many harebells, orchids and trefoil make bright the grassy acres. Here the crofters' cattle are pastured, for most of the machair is common grazing land. In charge of the beasts is usually a veteran *buachaille* or herdsman. One such I often saw. He 'had' little English, but his manners were courtly and dignified as of a chieftain, and his eye at times lit up with a proud eagle-like glance. A sentence spoken to him in indifferent Gaelic caused his fine face to light up with pleasure; one cannot approach the hearts of the Highland race unless one knows a little of their language.

The greatest event in the lives of the Uist and Barra crofters takes place in July, when the annual Highland gathering is held. In these days, when Highland games have elsewhere become social functions, where one meets one's friends but takes only a mild interest in the games themselves, it is refreshing to find a meeting like that of South Uist, where it is the games alone which attract the interest of the spectators. How keen everyone is!

The whole island turns up at the machair, with the clear sea water just beyond it. The natural turf is short and very green. The people line the ring. Scarcely a word of English is heard; the islanders talk animatedly amongst themselves in Gaelic. The young girls are smartly dressed in the height of fashion; the older women appear with their most snow-white shawls about their heads.

So enthusiastic are some that they actually cross from Benbecula (in their carts at low tide) the night before, and pass the hours of darkness out in the open, or prevail upon friends or relations — nearly everyone is related in the islands — to offer them hospitality. The games commence at 11am — that is, ten o'clock by the islanders' time, for summertime finds little favour in these remote parts — and it is half past eight in the evening before the last event has been decided.

In South Uist the great feature of the gathering is the piping. Considering that it is confined to local players the standard is probably higher than at any Scottish meeting upon the mainland. Certainly for its size South Uist has more pipers than any other district of the Highlands. How well they played when the emigrants left Lochboisdale that April Sunday of 1923 will always be remembered by those who heard them — but there were some upon the island who would not readily excuse them for tuning up their pipes upon the Sabbath.

The Uist gathering opens with a march, strathspey and reel competition, for which, on the occasion when I helped judge them, no fewer than eighteen pipers came forward. The first competitor is usually a trifle shy, but as the playing goes on this diffidence wears off, and much cheering at the close of a particularly good performance stimulates the remaining players to their keenest efforts.

After this competition has been decided, and the hard worked judges have been permitted to retire for a hurried lunch, the *Ceol Mor* or Big Music playing is decided. *Ceol Mor* is the classical music of the pipes, yet few pipers of the present generation have mastered it. It may be because of their loneliness and dreariness that the Islands produce the piping of dance music rather than the old tunes of mournful composition. Well played, and with the pipes going sufficiently well to last out the tune, *Ceol Mor*, or *piobaireachd* as it is generally called, is a thing of great beauty, and the tunes are the more interesting in that they are usually several hundred years old, one at least dating back to the thirteenth century.

Following close upon the piping there is much dancing of reels, and a number of competitors of both sexes enter for the *gille challum*, or sword dance, the 'swords' being two stout walking sticks laid across each other.

Tossing the 'cabar', or pole, attracts the most burly manhood of the islands. The 'cabar' is a formidable-looking tree trunk — it may be an ancient telegraph pole, for this is a treeless land — and for a considerable time proves too much for the competitors, only one of whom can so much as lift, let alone toss it! The pole must have several pieces sawn off it before the champion strongman of the island (an ex-pipe major of the Camerons) succeeds in tossing it, to the accompaniment of a roar of cheering. So scarce is wood upon the isle, it is humorously suggested that the sawn-off portions be awarded the unsuccessful competitors as consolation prizes!

But perhaps the greatest excitement is aroused by the pony race, for almost every crofter possesses a pony, and although they ride without saddle or bridle (a piece of rope takes the place of the latter), they cover the ground at a surprising speed, each one being cheered wildly by his own supporters. This race is held upon the wide sands, at low tide, and although other events are being decided at the same time, almost every spectator leaves the gathering ground for a point from which the sands may be viewed.

Towards evening blue smoke arises from peat fires on the machair beside the meeting place as some of the people from distant parts of the island brew their tea, yet the interest in the sports never flags, and it is a tired and happy crowd that witnesses the prize-giving in the late evening, and then commences its homeward journey in conveyances of all descriptions, or on foot.

It is now after nine o'clock, and away behind the Monach Islands the sun is sinking in a golden sky, where, upon the north-west horizon, crimson cumulus clouds float about St Kilda's highest peak, faint and needle-like above the Atlantic wastes. Some of the people from Benbecula have come twenty miles or more, and it must be past sunrise next morning when these travellers reach their homes after a crowded day that must give them frequent thought during the uneventful months to come. To those from Barra the journey is an even more difficult one, and at the gathering of which I write some of the best pipers of that island arrived late on the ground, having failed to obtain a boat in which to cross the wide Sound of Barra. No doubt the judges would have allowed them to play had not their modesty prevented them from making their presence known.

After the gathering there is much activity on Barra, for the herring fishing is then at its height, and boats assemble there from every part of Scotland.

The first rye grass is cut in the Outer Hebrides towards the end of July, lying for weeks in the fields before it is sufficiently dried to be harvested should the season be unfavourable.

The season of true harvest is dependent largely on the weather. The potatoes, oats and meadow hay are often gathered in together in October. All this harvesting is done by hand, and the potatoes are dug in a curious manner. The people kneel on the sandy soil, working up the drills. With a sickle-like implement they scrape away the sand from the roots of the plants, exposing the tubers, which they collect and place in a pail. During a wild October day with flurries of rain sweeping across from the Atlantic one sometimes sees men and women kneeling for hours in their small fields as they laboriously harvest the tubers which mean so much to them during the long winter months.

It is in autumn, when the west wind often blows almost continuously, that

South Uist becomes permeated with a curious smell, given off from the masses of seaweed that have been stranded along its western shore. It is not unpleasant, and on the wind is carried far inland; as one approaches the shore it becomes more insistent. There is another curious smell given off by the bog-lands when warmth and sunshine follow upon the heels of a prolonged rainy spell.

During one wild October day I chanced to pass by a small thatched cottage and, calling in to shelter awhile, found the house tenanted by a middle-aged woman and her mother. The old lady was well over ninety years of age, and shivered as she sat close up to the small fire of peat, for the day was a cold one. She had no word of English, but spoke continuously in Gaelic as she rocked herself on her chair. When younger she had done much weaving, and she showed me with pride a kilt of MacDonald tartan she had woven for one of her sons. Like the old herdsman she had that indefinable quality of refinement and good breeding so characteristic of the best type of West Highlander, and one could imagine she would have been at home in the most exalted circumstances, as in the most lowly.

The following summer, when the sun shone warm upon the machair, and the loch near her house, with its ruined castle, lay bathed in the mystic light of the west, I again visited the wee dwelling. The old lady was abed and failing fast. She crooned to herself as she lay upon the bed, and her voice was more feeble. Yet she spoke much, and seemed glad that my wife and I had come again to visit her. Especially glad, I remember, was she to greet our small daughter, whom she saw for the first time. At our parting she seemed to realise that we should not meet again, for she was greatly affected – holding our hands and speaking words of blessing and farewell. And even as we left the room and gained the doorway her words followed us: 'Beannachd, beannachd' (Blessings, blessings) were the two last words we heard, and I shall always remember them, and the simple dignity with which they were spoken. This old lady had lived out all her long life without ever leaving her native island.

There are now, as I have said, few *ceilidh*, or winter gatherings, where old traditions used to be handed down from one generation to another, and where the old beliefs and superstitions were perpetuated. One rarely, if ever, hears mention nowadays of the Blue Men (*Na Fir Gorma*). Tradition has it that the fallen angels were driven out of Paradise in three divisions. One became the fairies, another the Blue Men of the Ocean, while a third were transformed into the Aurora's pale shafts of light that play of a winter's night about the northern heavens. The Gaelic name for this third company is *Na Fir Chlis*, or the Agile Men. The Blue Men seem to have had their home chiefly in the waters of the Minch. The channel between Lewis and the Shiant Isles (*Na-h-eileanan siant*) is, or was, known as *Sruth nam Fear Gorm* – the Stream of the Blue Men. Here these supernatural people might be seen, of a moonlight night, to play a hotly contested game of shinty!

One April I sailed twice during the course of a single day through this Stream of the Blue Men. In the morning there was a stiff north-easter, and the hills of Harris were from time to time hidden in squalls of driving sleet. In the evening the wind had moderated, and as we sailed southward through the Sruth the rays of a young moon were cresting the waves with mellow light. East of us loomed darkly the Shiant Isles, west was the rugged coastline of Lewis. On the far eastern horizon across the Minch a great heather fire flared upon the hills of Ross. An hour before midnight the northern sky burned with a greenish glow. Soon, as I watched, pale shafts of light, as if from distant searchlights, began to play about the northern heavens. They flickered, died away, then shot upward once more. The Nimble Men were abroad, and perhaps, unseen by me, their cousins the Blue Men were cleaving the northerly swell as they swam and glided after the ball in their unending game of *camanachd*, or shinty.

Wherever one goes, throughout the length and breadth of the Long Island, one finds the old traditions and superstitions still lingering. They will long remain, for the people of the Isles live very close to Nature, and in her great forces they find inscrutable laws which are the origin of many of their strange beliefs.

But the spread of education has made the islanders rely less upon their memories, and it is a very rare thing nowadays to find a man who can relate by heart the tales of Ossian and his Heroes – there is much 'schooling' for the children, and upon leaving school they are eager to be off to Glasgow and other large towns, where their store of worldly knowledge is increased, but where they lose the simplicity, dignity and charming courtesy that mark the people of the Western Isles as a race apart.

So that, did they but know it, they may gain little, and lose that which money is unable to purchase.

CHAPTER XXI
A Hebridean Emigration

ON AUGUST 11th, 1851, great excitement and activity prevailed in the little Outer Hebridean harbour of Lochboisdale, South Uist. Four hundred and fifty islanders were being shipped to Quebec on board the good ship *Admiral*, and there was much lamenting on shore and upon the vessel, for some of the emigrants were 'up in years' as they say in the West, and, so it is narrated, were leaving their native island with extreme reluctance and even dismay.

Now, after all these years, Lochboisdale was this April morning of 1923 the scene of another great departure of islesmen for a far distant country. Over 300 men, women and children were being embarked on board the Canadian Pacific steamer *Marloch* for Red Deer Valley, Alberta, there to found a compact Gaelic-speaking colony.

The *Marloch*, a liner of just over 10,000 tons, was formerly known as the *Victorian*, and during the early years of the war was an armed merchant cruiser, one of the ships of Admiral Sir Reginald Tupper of the roving Tenth Cruiser Squadron. She was thus already familiar with the waters of the Minch, for her squadron had a wide patrol area of the west and north of Scotland, extending even up to the limits of the Polar ice fields. I was not unfamiliar with the *Victorian* on her occasional wartime visits to Loch Ewe in Western Ross; the senior Naval Officer at Aultbea was frequently up all night prior toher arrival to see that no lurking submarines had gained access to the loch. But in those days the *Marloch* was a man-of-war; now she has returned to her original duty as a passenger liner.

There is, I think, no doubt that she is the largest vessel that has ever anchored off Lochboisdale, and this fact alone would have brought all the island population of South Uist to the pier-head to view her — even apart from the intense excitement which the great emigration scheme aroused.

The emigrants were drawn from a district full of historical associations. Near Lochboisdale is the island of Eriskay, set in the Sound of Barra, where Prince Charles Edward first landed on his romantic voyage from France in 1745 in order to endeavour to persuade the Highland chiefs and chieftains to support his cause.

Then, again, Lochboisdale is almost beneath the shadow of Corodale, where the prince was sheltered in a remote cave a year later (the redcoats being all the while close on his track) after his final defeat at Culloden. From Corodale Bonnie Prince Charlie was spirited by Flora MacDonald across the Minch to Skye in the guise of an Irish maidservant, and under the name of Betty Burke.

All through the night the *Marloch* had steered north-west from the Clyde. She had seen the last of the sunset die slowly behind Rathlin Island, and the light-houses of Islay and Skerryvore had guided her on her passage. The night was calm, with a following southerly breeze. Before sunrise the Hebrides were sight-ed, but long before the first of the dawn the powerful light on Barra Head had stabbed the soft darkness of this April night. The sunrise was a fine one, and we steamed northward at fifteen knots in ideal weather and through a smooth sea. The more southern of the Hebrides were passed in quick succession. Mingulay, with its sheer, even overhanging precipices of over 800ft, where countless sea fowl nest, soon dropped astern. Now we were abreast of Pabbay and Vatersay, and a few minutes later Barra Island with its conical hill Heaval was close to us.

Last of all, before we made South Uist, the sands of Eriskay gleamed in the golden sunlight.

Bird life was plentiful this spring morning. Flying low above the sea, strings of guillemots and razorbills were steering for Mingulay. The islanders counted their early arrival a favourable omen for a fine summer. Solan geese, singly and in pairs, crossed our bows, flying with surprising grace and with unhurried flight, and steering by way of the Sound of Barra to their nesting cliffs upon far distant St Kilda. Their course was thus at right angles to that of the guillemots and razor-bills, but each species of bird flew unhesitatingly, although its destination was out of sight.

A few Manx shearwaters dipped and banked with their characteristic progress, but the puffins had not yet arrived upon their summer waters.

Shortly after seven o'clock we steamed slowly in towards South Uist, anchoring about a mile off the entrance to Lochboisdale. We had many passengers aboard – Canadians, Scotsmen and Englishmen – and they gazed curiously upon the desolate isle which most of them had never seen, or perhaps even heard of, before. And in truth the isle seemed dreary in the extreme. From the anchorage of the liner not a house could be seen, not a field relieved the desolate aspect of the country. The grass as yet was brown as in midwinter; with various shades of brown – grass, heather and bracken – the hills were covered. How could a stranger know that a first appearance is deceptive, and that along the west side of the isle there is fertile machair land, with many crofting townships?

Until close on midday we remained at anchor without a sign of human life on shore or at sea, but at midday the small steamer *Dunara Castle* – which on this occasion was acting as 'tender' to the *Marloch* – hove in sight to the southward. She brought the emigrants from Barra, just one hundred in all – a service had been held on that island previous to her departure, during which the wanderers had been blessed in their great undertaking – and was soon alongside. On board the smaller ship one heard much Gaelic talk, and from the liner as she towered above the tender one could see something of the emigrants as they gazed upward uncertainly at what, to them, must have appeared a vessel of incredible proportions. There were one or two men of sixty or thereabouts, with fine open faces, bearded and deeply bronzed, but the majority were considerably younger. Their wives and families accompanied them — anxious-faced women with headgear of shawls of various colours, white, brown, or tartan. It seemed sad that Scotland should be unable to provide a home for these simple and dignified island families, with the blood of the old Highland chiefs in their veins, and one could not but pity them because of the long transatlantic voyage and the immense railway journey of 2800 miles at its close. These settlers were destined to find their future homes in Alberta, almost under the shadow of the Rocky Mountains, so that although they were leaving their well-loved sea they would still have the hills to inspire them. To the head of each family 160 acres of land had been allotted — virgin land which may have to be cleared with much hard labour, but capable of yielding a good return in the course of a year or two.

It was early afternoon when the Dunara Castle, which, by the way, has for half a century been one of the institutions of the Western Isles, approached the pier at Lochboisdale in order to pick up the emigrants who had assembled there from the islands of South Uist and Benbecula. Fully 1500 persons were on or beside the pier; nothing like such a concourse had ever before been seen upon the island. We landed the medical officer of the Board of Trade to inspect the emigrants, and gradually 200 of them were stowed away on board the small steamship.

The sun shone with summer heat; one or two of the children at the landing place had discarded shoes and stockings. A piper discoursed cheerful music upon the pier; on the blue waters of the loch a freshening wind was forming white wavelets. Many miles to the east, hazy and ethereal in the strong sunlight, stood the island of Rhum with its conical peaks, and northward of it the serrated summits of the Cuchulain Hills of Skye.

It must have been an added sorrow to the islanders to leave their relatives, friends and simple homes on a day such at this. One heard many tearful farewells, all of them in the Gaelic tongue. 'Beannachd leat' (Blessings be with you) one heard constantly, spoken with trembling accents. But, the short farewell said, these simple and very charming people kept a smiling and cheerful face towards the land that some of the older people were in all probability looking on for the last time in this life.

Nothing but stern necessity could force these Hebridean crofters and cottars to emigrate; yet more will soon follow, for it is difficult to see how they can earn a living on the islands of their birth. Each summer of late has been more inclement than the last; in October I have seen the hay still in the fields and the oats uncut.

A Reverend Father of Barra who, full of cheerfulness and enthusiasm, was accompanying his people to Alberta, informed me in the course of conversation that the persistent fishing of trawlers within the three-mile limit has been a very serious thing for the islanders. Recently trawlers have penetrated even into the Sound of Barra, and have dragged their trawls over the spawning beds of the flounders, causing irretrievable damage. It is suggested that, instead of confiscating the ship's gear and fining the master £100, his certificate, in cases of proved illegal trawling, should be cancelled. This undoubtedly would prove an effective deterrent.

It was late afternoon before the last of the emigrants boarded the tender, and the last of their personal belongings were hoisted into the hold. South Uist has many excellent pipers, and one of them who was making the long overseas journey played such animated marches as 'MacDonald of Glencoe' and 'The Highland Wedding', pacing up and down the after-part of the vessel. On shore a second piper was playing in time with the first. As the *Dunara Castle* cast off her moorings there was a sudden fluttering of handkerchiefs. Cheer after cheer was sent after the vessel by those on shore, cheer after cheer was returned across the water.

Up to now nothing except cheerful pipe music had been heard. But as the boat slipped out across the waters of Lochboisdale one of the older men seized his pipes and the very mournful strains of an old Gaelic air seemed to voice the sorrow of that company of wanderers. The pipes were not in tune, the execution did not compare with that of the previous players, yet that sad melody will always remain in my mind, for it was obviously played from a heart that was heavy with sorrow.

The wind was freshening; something of the forebodings of the emigrants seemed to have entered into the weather itself. The air was chill; the sun's rays failed to warm the heather-clad banks of the loch. A party of handsome eider drakes with their attendant ducks of sober plumage flew rapidly downwind over Lochboisdale, unmindful of the great gathering of people on the shore. Just about this time two ravens circled overhead, and I wondered if some of the older people had seen them, and had taken an omen from their presence. The raven from earliest times was carried by the chiefs of the Isles upon their voyages of exploration and thus it seemed fit that a pair of these birds of wisdom should wheel above this emigrant ship.

Beyond the shelter of the loch the sea was momentarily rising. The liner was unaffected by the short waves, but the small *Dunara Castle* was pitching to such an extent that it was impossible to disembark the settlers. And so a number of miserable hours were passed, the women and children prostrate with sickness. It was not until sunset that the wind moderated, and the transhipment could be effected. In the twilight a great heather fire blazed from the slopes of Beinn Ruigh Choinnich, glowing fiercely as each gust caught it, almost dying away in the succeeding calm. In the air was the pleasant smell of burning peats and of burning heather, and through it, unobserved, the liner *Marloch* sailed southward to round Barra Head and steer west for her far distant destination of St John, New Brunswick.*

* Just a week later I watched at Stornoway the embarkation of some 300 emigrants for Canada on board the CPR liner Metagama.

PART IV
Some Birds of the Hebrides

CHAPTER XXII
The Twite, or Mountain Linnet

WHILE THE common or brown linnet is a bird known to most observers the same cannot be said for the slightly smaller mountain linnet or twite.

Like the dunlin, this cheery little finch has entirely different habits in various parts of Scotland. In the central Highlands, for instance, it is a bird of the high hills, nesting 3000ft above the sea, with the dotterel and the ptarmigan as its companions. But upon the windy Hebrides it has its summer home at sea level, and upon the island of South Uist takes the place of the house sparrow, which is unknown there.

In length the twite is five inches – about half an inch shorter than the common linnet – and although the two resemble each other somewhat, the common linnet may be distinguished by having each tail feather margined with white, and by the patch of red on the forehead and flanks. The most striking characteristic of the twite, in the Outer Hebrides at all events, is its remarkable fearlessness. In the large walled garden of the lodge where we lived at least a dozen pairs of twites nested. They and the larks were the only songbirds we had, and no matter how wet and stormy the day, they sang cheerily – and always on the wing. These little birds seem to be resident on the islands. They form into flocks at the approach of winter, haunting the stack-yards of the crofters, where they shelter as best they may, and feed on the small seeds among the grain.

When we arrived at the lodge on April 25th, a pair of twites had completed their small nest in a bush within a dozen feet of the front door. Although there was much sunshine about that time, the wind was bitterly cold, and it was not until May 7th that the first egg was found in the nest.

Four fragile eggs of a sky-blue colour, spotted sparingly with red-brown, were laid, and after the fourth had been deposited the birds – for both cock and hen shared in the brooding – commenced to sit. So far as I am aware, the incubation period of the twite had never before been determined and as this nest was in an ideal place for observation it was visited daily. So tame did the hen become, she used to allow us to feel the eggs beneath her without rising from the nest. In eleven and a half days (a very short period) the young were hatched.

To make more certain that this was the usual period of incubation a second nest – perhaps belonging to the same pair of birds – was watched later in the season. On June 18th the first egg was laid; on the 21st the fourth and last was deposited, and the birds commenced to sit. This nest hatched twelve days later — on July 3rd. On the 17th, after just a fortnight, the young were fully fledged, and when I peered into the bush two flew off. The remaining chicks did not leave the nest for two days, pointing to a somewhat prolonged period of fledging for birds which are hatched out so speedily.

I believe almost every pair of twites rear two families in the season. It is possible that three broods are produced at times, for as late as July 25th, I saw a twite with a feather in her bill, and on the 30th of that month I found a nest with newly-hatched young.

The nesting sites of the South Uist twites varied greatly. Where bushes and stunted trees were present — they are very rare upon that windswept spot, and there is not a tree of respectable size upon the island — the little mountain linnets nested in them, at a height of from three to eight feet above the ground. Even gorse is a rare and imported plant in the island; in only one place did I see it growing to any size, and here twites were nesting in the bushes. In the garden of the lodge a row of stunted shrubs grew up against the wall of the house. Here at least half a dozen pairs of twites nested, two to four feet above the ground. In the wall which surrounded the garden were one or two crannies, which were occupied with nests; but the wall was so well and substantially built that few nesting sites were available in it.

The birds also nested sparingly about the shores of the moorland lochs, among the long heather and rocks at the water's edge. The nests usually resembled those of the true linnet, hut were scarcely so tidy, and there was not so much wool in the lining.

The twites lived chiefly upon the western or machair side of the island, which is the most populous part. They never frequented the hills themselves. When first thinking of nesting, both cock and hen birds were engrossed in searching for a suitable nesting site. The male twite is a model husband, and, when the nest had been commenced, he accompanied his lady on each occasion that she flew home with nesting material, remaining perched on the bush in close attendance, and hurrying off after his mate when she left the nest. When the young were in danger from prowling cats both birds showed signs of the most acute distress, and welcomed the arrival of the human intruder.

The young twites for the first few days were naked little objects, but grew fast. They were fed upon seeds, which were disgorged by their parents on arriving at the nest and thrust far down the hungry young throats. The visits of the parent twites to the nest were at intervals of half an hour, both cock and hen arriving together. Most small birds visit their young much more frequently, but it must be remembered that a whinchat, or, let us say, a flycatcher, carrying perhaps a single grub or caterpillar, feeds each chick every five minutes or so, whereas a twite, arriving every' half-hour, produces an incredible number of seeds, and may feed the whole brood at a single visit. Between their journeys to their young, one could seethe parent twites busily pulling the seeds — and even the flowers themselves for the rudiments of seeds which they contained — from the dandelion plants.

The song of the twite is not ambitious. It is a cheery warble, and, as I have mentioned before, is uttered almost always upon the wing. The male twite rises a little way into the air, sailing earthward with curious and very distinctive flight and singing the while. No storm is too fierce, no rain is too heavy, to damp his ardour. During the whole of that memorably cold and rough spring and early summer of 1922 the twite's song was rarely absent; I used to see him from my window going through his aerial flight and music when rain in sheets drove in upon the arms of a south-westerly gale from the leaden Atlantic on the horizon. The roughness of the elements often spoilt the effect of his graceful little earthward dive, for he had to fight hard to keep his balance, but he was always an invincible optimist — as all must be to enjoy the climate of the Hebrides.

Affection, cheeriness, fearlessness. These are three fine qualities, and the character of the twite, or mountain linnet, should be an object lesson to us all.

CHAPTER XXIII
The Dunlin

OF ALL the shore birds that frequent the coasts of Britain during the months of autumn and winter none is more feverishly active than the dunlin. It is a charming sight to watch a flock of these small waders — in size the dunlin is rather less than a snipe — as they feed at the edge of the tide. Each receding wave they follow up, wading thigh-deep and probing the soft sand with their long sensitive bills. Back they speed just ahead of the next oncoming wave which threatens to engulf them. They may be able to outdistance it on foot, but as often as not are compelled to take wing to escape the advancing flood. Of the marvellous unison in which they wheel, swerve, and double back in their collective flight many have written — how each individual of the flock appears to be under the influence of an impulse common to all.

With the coming of May the tidal shores know the dunlin no more, for the little birds are then scattering far and wide to their nesting grounds. Some fly no farther than the Scottish Highlands, others range north to Greenland, Spitsbergen, and Siberia. This is the age of the minute subdivision of birds, and amongst ornithologists three subspecies of dunlin are recognised.

The first of these (*Erolia alpina alpina*) nests in Northern Norway and Sweden, Finland, Lapland, North Russia, and West Siberia. It is slightly larger than the British nesting dunlin. The second subspecies is named *Erolia alpina schinzii*. This variety has its nesting haunts on the southern shores of the Baltic, in Southern Sweden, Denmark and the British Islands. The most northerly nesting dunlin appears to be *Erolia alpina arctica*, very closely resembling our own dunlin. This subspecies nests in Greenland, and seemingly it is the form found in Spitsbergen, where a few colonies breed.

But even in the British Isles themselves it has often seemed to me that two races of dunlin must exist, for the habits of this quaint little bird are so distinct in different districts. In central Scotland, for example, the dunlin is a bird of the hill plateaux, nesting usually between 2500 and 3000ft above the sea. But in the Western Highlands I have never met with it on the hills, even those a few hundred feet high; it nests in boggy ground fringing the lochs of Hebridean islands almost at sea level, and is quite absent from the moorlands.

In South Uist the dunlin nests in large numbers, and during the spring and summer of 1922 I was able to gather some interesting information on their nesting habits. As far as could be determined the first pair of dunlin arrived on April 30th at the nesting ground, where later on several dozen pairs might be seen daily. Thus the interesting fact was brought out that these birds, like so many other of our summer visitors, are paired before arriving at the nesting haunt.

On the next day (May 1st) some redshank were heard calling, near the dunlins' nesting haunt, but they must have passed on; they do not seem to nest anywhere on South Uist.

From April 30th until May 11th the pair of dunlin had the bog to themselves, but on the latter day a flock of these birds were observed to circle above the nesting ground. On the following day they were busy pegging out their territory along the shore of the loch, and one pair had already commenced their nesting 'scrapes'. On May 16th, after much heavy rain, these 'scrapes' were under water, and a mute swan nesting near was forced by the rising of the loch to abandon her eggs. On May 19th the first dunlin's completed nest was found. It contained three eggs, but the bird had not begun to sit. This nest was in a tussock of grass in a moderately dry situation. On the 21st of the month two more nests were discovered. They each contained four eggs, pear-shaped and very beautifully marked, and their owners had begun to brood them. On May 26th a turf 'hide' was commenced near one of the nests, a few sods being cut at intervals so as not unduly to disturb the birds. The hiding-place was completed on the 29th, a depressing day, with strong southerly breeze and thick fog.

On the morning of June 1st the incessant wind died away. All through May it had blown from west or south-west without a break, day and night. A curious result of this wind was that no dew fell, and when the wind was unaccompanied by rain, the ground became parched and dry in a remarkably short space of time. Thus it was very pleasant to be abroad in a calm, and to see the loch unruffled and tranquil. Early in the morning I made my way to the 'hide'. From the rushes which fringed the loch a scaup duck left her hiding-place. As she swam agitatedly on the loch, her white forehead — it is only by this that the female scaup may be distinguished from the female tufted duck — was very noticeable through the glass. She was soon joined by her mate, in handsome black and white plumage. Swimming quietly across the loch, a shoveller duck appeared; a pair of scoters floated together.

The dunlin was by now indifferent to the turf hide, and soon after I had been shut inside by my wife the bird returned to the nest, running quietly through the withered grass — the young grass was even now scarcely showing, so backward was the spring. On the occasion when the nest was first found the dunlin flew straight from her eggs, but subsequently she ran from her nest, never showing herself, so that at first we feared lest the eggs were deserted. Her behaviour was probably influenced by a pair of oystercatchers, which had their nest with four eggs — an unusually large number — on the shore of the loch near. These oystercatchers were of exceptionally nervous, or fussy disposition, and flew around, with shrill and repeated whistling whenever a person appeared in sight. Even when they had eggs they were demonstrative; in June, when their four downy nestlings were hatched, the clamour of the parents was deafening.

A rare bird passed near the dunlin's nesting ground one day about this time. In size it resembled the herring gull, but its wings lacked the dark primary feathers, and I recognised it as that dweller of the ice-locked fjords of snowy Spitsbergen – the glaucous gull. This wanderer from Polar regions seemed tired; it progressed in short flights, moving just above the surface of the ground.

Several days were spent in the 'hide' photographing and observing the dunlin.

Of these June 7th was perhaps the finest. A strong southerly breeze ruffled the loch, but its breath was unusually warm. From afar the scent of innumerable wild hyacinths was carried on the wind; about the water dragonflies of many sizes and brilliant colouring darted. Phalaropes chased each other above the sedges. Larks poured out a flood of joyous music from the azure fields of the almost cloudless sky. In the fields the first corncrake was heard; on a bush there perched an almost white corn bunting. By now dunlin were nesting everywhere, and common gulls, as I have mentioned in another chapter, were most troublesome to them, constantly searching for their well-hidden eggs, which they regarded as a special dainty.

To one who knows the dunlin only as a winter bird, the handsome plumage which it assumes during the nesting season must be a revelation. The breast is now a striking black – this black breast is assumed also by other 'waders', such as the golden and grey plover, during their nesting – and the whole plumage is more handsomely marked.

On June 10th the dunlin's eggs were chipping, and the following day the young had left the nest, nor could a trace be found of them or of the parent birds. One could but hope they had escaped the clutches of the many common gulls. The eggs, when first found, were quite fresh, so that the incubation period was just twenty-one days. On the same day (June 11th) the young of the oystercatchers hatched out also, and they certainly escaped an untimely end, for they were seen on several occasions subsequently. Between June 11th and 21st dunlins' nests were hatching out everywhere. The very small chicks are active from the first, and are able to run quickly and to hide amongst the grass, their chocolate-coloured down of considerable thickness being in harmony with the vegetation.

The absence of young grass until so late in the summer was doubtless very much against them, for it rendered them more conspicuous to the marauding gulls. Indeed, in some parts there was scarcely any cover at all, even by mid-June. Some of those dunlin which had lost their eggs laid second clutches, and as late as June 25th I saw a nest containing two fresh eggs.

On July 9th, I saw the first young dunlin able to fly; a gnome-like, ungainly little bird it looked as it took wing. By now many of those dunlin which had failed to rear broods were already in small flocks, flying restlessly about the lochs or feeding in the soft ooze on the shores.

Full summer was now come to the Hebrides. In the lochs heavy trout swam lazily to the surface, sucking down the swarms of gnats which hatched off after a spell of warm sunshine unaccompanied by wind. By now the corncrake had cover in plenty in which to 'crek'. On the waters the mute swans swam proudly, their cygnets beside them. Curlew were already arriving on the island from their nesting grounds on the mainland to the east; from the sand-dunes whimbrel called.

Each day from now onward the dunlin became fewer at their nesting grounds. This gradual decrease could be seen clearly on the shores of a large loch near the north end of the island. Here nested hundreds of pairs of dunlin; all May and June the gnome-like birds had circled round one agitatedly or else had run quickly ahead of the human trespasser, uttering quaint cries with little melody in them, though of a distinctive charm. It was interesting to note that all the larks imitated the dunlins' guttural alarm note in their songs.

In July the behaviour of the dunlin changed. The majority had lost their young; the minority had hatched and reared their broods; indeed, the percentage of young birds which escaped the hoofs of grazing cattle or the ravages of gulls must have been a very low one. On July 31st only a very few dunlin now remained at their chief nesting ground. These had already lost the handsome black breast of the nesting plumage. By now young and old could be distinguished only with difficulty; yet even at this late date there were still a few young dunlin scarcely able to fly. It would be of interest to know how far south the dunlin of the Outer Hebrides range after the nesting season, and how quickly they made their southward flight. In winter the species is found south to the Mediterranean region and North Africa. It occurs west to the Canaries, while in the East it is distributed through the Red Sea to Zanzibar and Mozambique.

I think that many young dunlins might be saved in those crofting districts of the Outer Hebrides where cattle are pastured near the lochs, by fencing off here and there a strip of grass near the water's edge. This would be beneficial in two ways; it would prevent the cattle breaking the eggs or crushing the chicks, and it would, by allowing the grass to grow, provide cover against the attacks of the common gulls. And the areas enclosed need not be so large as to interfere materially with grazing. Yet I fear in these hard times no landowner could afford this, nor are the various Bird Protection Societies sufficiently rich for such an undertaking. So the little dunlin and red-necked phalarope must be left to fight their own battles for existence against the cattle, the common gulls, and the wind and rain.

CHAPTER XXIV
The Lesser Tern

THE TRIBE of the sea swallows are not plentiful upon South Uist. Not plentiful, that is to say, when one takes into consideration the great stretch of sandy beach that extends the whole length of the island, along its western side. But there is at least one colony of this quaint and agile bird, and that is near the north end of the isle, close beside where a little stream — or *sruth* as it is termed in the Gaelic — enters the emerald waters of the Atlantic. Here, when May is come, the little tern commences to arrive, moving up the coast from the south, and fishing daintily as it goes.

But surely no birds can have been so unlucky with their nesting as the lesser terns that I watched one season. The weather was wintry when the colony arrived in May.

During June wild storms and stinging squalls swept the lonely shore; it was not until late July that any decided improvement took place. And all this time the lesser terns were endeavouring — and without success — to raise their broods.

It was June 19th when I visited the colony for the first time. At that date there were about twenty pairs of birds. Of those some twelve pairs were nesting; the remainder stood below high-water mark, or else fished gracefully for sand eels along the line of breaking surf. The brooding terns were very tame, and by lying amongst the sand dunes I was able to mark down a number of the birds as they returned to their eggs. There is usually no nest; the two eggs are laid on the sand in a very slight depression scraped by the bird.

On this day one of the so-called nests contained no fewer than four eggs. This is an altogether remarkable number for a lesser tern; in fact, I doubt if it has ever before been recorded, and it is possible that two hens may have laid together. Amongst the colony were two pairs of Arctic terns, noticeable by their larger size and longer and more graceful wings and by the absence of the white forehead.

The weather was rough and very unsettled, but on the morning of June 23rd it cleared, and the wind at last fell away to a light breeze from the north. Early that morning I put up a hiding-tent at the tern's nesting ground, and after breakfast moved it up near to the nest containing four eggs. The weather was clear, and the sea calm. Some distance beyond the line of minute waves that broke upon the sands a dark object appeared on the Atlantic. It looked for all the world like a small boat, and I wondered to whom it might belong. But a 'spy' through a telescope proved it to be no boat, but a large grey seal balanced – precariously, so it seemed – upon a small rock that was just awash. Upon the north-west horizon the distant Monach Lighthouse showed, needle-like. Eastward, far beyond the flower-scented machair, the three big hills of Uist were of a deep blue, with mist about their tops. I was left in the hide by my wife, and the lesser tern returned, with little delay, to her eggs. I was interested to see whether she had any difficulty in covering her large clutch, but she brooded her four eggs without effort.

It was not until July 1 that I revisited the colony. In the interval there had been many wet and stormy days, and the previous night a gale, accompanied by heavy rain, had raged, moderating at 9.30am. All the lesser terns' nests, with one exception, had vanished!

By July 8th a number of the terns had laid again. The day was calm, but during the night half a gale from the north sprang up quickly, and in the morning the dry sand was being drifted along the shore like driven snow. Doubtless sitting on one's eggs under such conditions is an unpleasant occupation, and the terns showed little disposition to return to their nest. There was a lochan a few yards inland, and here the lesser terns fished, diving down upon the minnows and small fry which swam imprisoned in the small pools that were fast drying up. It was noted, however, that the terns hunted for long before diving at a single minnow, although the pools seemed alive with small fish. A few days later the lochan became completely dried up and I wondered what was the fate of all the small minnows, and whether it might be possible for them to exist in the wet mud until the autumn rains should have replenished the pool. Certainly the terns lost a valuable fishing ground.

During the previous occasions on which I had photographed the lesser terns the 'hide' had, in the first instance, been set up some distance away from the nest to be photographed, being moved up nearer after an interval of a few hours when the birds had acquired confidence. But on July 16th I was accompanied by two companions instead of one, and the extra person seemed to confuse the terns, for – although the hide was put up straight away only six feet from the nest I wished to photograph – when my companions had moved off the tern flew back without hesitation. The hiding-tent was made of canvas which harmonised closely with the light-coloured sand, and was plentifully camouflaged with seaweed. In the front of the hiding-tent three small slits permitted me to watch without being seen from outside, and through a larger slit the lens of the camera projected a short distance. To the bird photographer the hiding of the lens is usually a more troublesome problem than his own adequate concealment, and it is a good plan to leave a bottle in the slit overnight, as this has the same appearance as a lens, and accustoms the bird to the eye-like thing menacing it.

At 12.55pm I was left in the hide by my two companions, and almost at once the hen lesser tern flew down and covered her two eggs. She brooded them till

2.05pm, when, with much twittering, the cock, a bird of more handsome plumage, settled on the shingle a few yards away, and the hen was persuaded to turn the eggs over to his care. At 3.20pm, after he had been sitting for an hour and a quarter, the hen returned and took his place, but after a further forty minutes the cock returned once more and was brooding when I concluded my vigil half an hour later.

To so nervous and restless a bird as the lesser tern the hatching of the eggs must be a boring process, and so it was interesting to observe what short spells each bird took on the eggs at a time.

July 22nd was a beautiful windless day, and very warm. Rising just above the far horizon the topmost peak of St Kilda showed, some sixty miles away. Eastward, toward Skye, black thunderclouds were piled up, and from time to time the summit of Beinn Mhor was hidden.

The hide was still in position beside the nest, but only one egg now remained; the other had hatched out. A small lesser tern chick was running about on the shore near, and this youngster I placed in the nest, thinking it belonged to my pair of terns. Soon after I had been left in the hide by my wife, the tern came back, and I was surprised to see another chick run up from a different direction and go to it. Evidently I had placed the wrong chick in the nest!

A pair of house-hunting ringed plover – they are sometimes very late nesters – had betrayed a mild interest in the first chick, and had nearly 'mothered' it before the tern's arrival. The tern at first brooded both chicks and its remaining egg, but the little stranger seemed to realise the bird was not its rightful mother, and, suddenly breaking away, to the annoyance of its foster parent, ran with astonishing speed out of my view. Soon a second tern, evidently the proper parent, appeared, having at last tracked down its errant offspring, and calm was restored.

The hen bird I had under observation brooding on the small chick and unhatched egg was presently relieved by the cock, and as she walked off the nest she picked up pieces of seaweed and threw them over her shoulder. On an island in Liefde Bay, in the extreme north of Spitsbergen, I had seen a hen turnstone do almost exactly the same thing. Can it be, I wonder, that this curious and very pretty habit is a relic of a time when these birds covered their eggs on leaving them? More probably it is done from playfulness, or from light-heartedness because an irksome task is ended for a while.*

After a very few minutes the hen returned with a minute sand eel, which the chick took quickly from her and swallowed instantly. Previously the chick had asked the cock for food; he, however, had temporised by touching the youngster's bill with his own. The tide was near the full, and a heavy surf boomed continuously only a few yards from the hiding-tent, while from an almost unclouded sky the sun shone with great power.

* Recently, when photographing a curlew at the nest, the same thing was noticed.

Almost daily, and often for hours at a stretch, the cattle that were pastured on the machair were herded to the little burn beside the tern's colony, and many of the eggs were trampled upon. But still more harm was done, quite unconsciously, by the old herdsman, who sat about near the terns, keeping them off their nests. This of itself would have done little damage, but the crafty and wicked common gulls seized this opportunity of pouncing upon any unguarded egg or young chick and making a meal of it, quite regardless of the proximity of the herdsman.

Thus it came about that on July 23rd very few eggs or tern chicks remained. On this, perhaps the warmest day of the whole summer, I saw a new bird visitor – an Arctic skua, at the colony. This bold sea robber of dusky plumage was in hot pursuit of a raven, but was itself set upon by an angry lesser tern. In the shallow water a seal splashed vigorously, and at this a crowd of terns hurried to the scene. A common gull, passing by, impudently swooped and carried off a young lesser tern, gulping it own as it flew! The following day I saw almost the last tern chick devoured in this manner.

On July 27th, I again passed by the nesting ground of the lesser tern. A westerly gale had brought in an exceptionally high tide, and seaweed lay strewn all along the shore.

From the burn a large flock of ringed plover rose; oystercatchers followed each receding wave. But of all the colony of lesser terns not one single bird remained, for the last eggs and the last chicks had disappeared, and so the company had flown southwards, having failed, as far as my observations went, to rear one single young bird in the whole season!

Let us hope every summer is not so disastrous to this eminently graceful and charming bird of our sandy shores.

CHAPTER XXV
The Common Gull

IT IS curious that the term 'common' should be applied to a seagull which is certainly not the most abundant in these Islands. The black-headed gull is more plentiful by far — taking Britain as a whole — and I should say the herring gull was more numerous. The name may have arisen from the fact that in winter the common gull superficially resembles the black-headed species, which in winter loses its black head, and thus the two originally may have been classed together as 'common'. It is, doubtless, also frequently confounded with the kittiwake.

As a matter of fact the common gull does not nest in England, and in Scotland is confined largely to the more western districts. It nests, but not plentifully, in western Aberdeenshire, and here it seeks out the highest hill lochs, where its only companions are the ptarmigan, on whose eggs it preys. But in western Scotland it does not appear to nest far inland, and may be found from April until July upon most of the grassy islands in the sea lochs of Argyll. In the Outer Hebrides, where it is common, it nests mainly upon small islands in freshwater lochs.

The common gull frequents the Scottish coasts throughout the year, although it is probable that those individuals seen in December and January are visitors from the Norwegian fjords. It is early March before the Scottish nesting birds arrive, and when first seen they are invariably in flocks, making their presence heard by much clamour.

The gulls commenced to nest in Uist toward the end of April, and on the 29th of the month on a small island of an inland loch five nests, each with a single egg, were found.

These eggs had apparently all been laid that morning, and perhaps two dozen more nests were completed and ready for eggs. The following day, on a small island upon a loch nearer the Atlantic no common gull had as yet laid; thus it was interesting to see that each little colony had its own date for commencing to nest, and that the last-mentioned colony was just four days later in laying than the one which commenced on April 29th. In the Outer Hebrides the common gulls were, curiously enough, considerably in advance of the black-headed gulls — which were more locally distributed — in laying, although I should say that in most districts the reverse is the case.

During the first days of June, in unsettled weather, a hiding-tent was set up on an island where many pairs of common gulls were nesting, and on June 10th my wife and I rowed out to the island, moving the hide to within a dozen feet of one of the nests. Into the hiding-tent I went, and having fixed up my camera, was left by my wife, who rowed quickly away from the island. The gull colony, already accustomed to the tent, and not realizing that a human being lay concealed within, returned to their nests with no delay. The bird whose nest was only a few feet from me was no exception, and having brooded her three dark eggs unconcernedly for a few minutes, she had the fright of her life when I fired off the shutter of my camera at her. Jumping into the air, she alighted at a respectable distance, often uttering her alarm note. But to her surprise none of the colony paid the least attention to her — they evidently thought she had an attack of 'nerves' — so she soon returned to her nest.

The next time the shutter was released she took but little notice, and soon disregarded its noise. On one occasion she, of her own accord, left the nest and walking a little distance away picked up a straw in her bill. She returned sedately with it, and placed it in position by her eggs, though these were on the point of hatching. All around me were gulls, some brooding their eggs, others standing on guard near their mates or at the water's edge. Two of the company had a pitched battle beside the hide, to the accompaniment of much shrill screaming — though the colony as a whole showed but little interest in the combat.

Besides the gulls there was other and varied bird life on this small island. A mute swan had her large nest with its six eggs in the outlying reeds. At the water's edge the nest of a dunlin was artfully concealed in the quickly growing grass. On the drier ground an oystercatcher was endeavouring to hatch a solitary egg, and in a clump of rushes a tufted duck brooded her seven olive-coloured eggs.

As I watched, a pair of red-breasted mergansers swam up to the island. Clambering out of the water on to the stones only a few yards from my place of concealment, they dried and preened their feathers carefully. The merganser is one of the last birds to nest, and apparently the duck had not commenced to brood. Perhaps a hundred yards out into the loch a pair of scoters swam, the drake handsome in his jet-black plumage with yellow bill, the duck unobtrusive and subdued in colour.

On June 15th — five days later — I was again hidden away in my tent. The day was the most brilliant of the whole summer. The loch lay with almost unruffled surface; from a cloudless sky the sun shone warmly. Most of the young gulls were just hatching out, and in the nest before which my tent was pitched were three downy chicks, harmonizing very closely indeed with their surroundings. The parent bird, as before, returned without delay, and brooded her young family contentedly. After a time one of the youngsters, apparently finding the heat beneath his mamma's feathers too oppressive, insisted upon remaining outside the nest, although his mother made several efforts to persuade him to return to her.

After about an hour the parent bird with some difficulty disgorged a black, sticky substance, which the young one pecked at and ate. It seemed to me to be half-digested insects, and certainly insect life was unusually abundant upon the loch on this day. The cock bird on one occasion alighted at the edge of the nest beside his mate, and there was much conversation in a loud, high-pitched key.

The young gulls grew apace. The dunlins had hatched off their brood on the island, but the chicks had disappeared mysteriously, and it was about this time that the common gulls developed criminal habits.

On the soft grassy ground beside the loch many dunlins were nesting, and a number of lapwings on the drier parts. Whenever a herdsman passed, or whenever a pedestrian used the old road, now grass-grown, that led across the machair, the dunlins and lapwings, too, were disturbed from their nests or young broods. Now was the opportunity of the marauding common gulls. On seeing a person cross the machair the gulls would converge upon him and accompany him, flying near him, but a little ahead. In this way they were able to mark the dunlins as they left their eggs or youngsters, and, with the greatest impudence, would then swoop quickly down, devour the eggs at a gulp, or carry off a chick, to swallow it in the air. On one occasion, when two of us were sitting at a loch side, within twenty yards of where a dunlin had her nest with four hard-set eggs, a common gull shot down and before we had realised what was happening bolted the four eggs, one after another, in as many seconds.

The more we saw of the common gulls, the more we became convinced that their diet in June and the earlier part of July consisted almost entirely of the eggs and chicks of other birds. The lapwings did their best to drive off the criminals, but their attacks lacked method, and in the end they, too, not infrequently had their eggs and young carried off.

In another chapter I have told how the common gulls daily, almost hourly, harried a colony of lesser terns.

Here, in Uist, they were certainly the most destructive of the gull tribe, although the herring and lesser black-backed gull nested commonly, and a number of pairs of great black backs were present also. And yet the common gull is dove-like in appearance! Although a considerable colony of black-headed gulls nested on an island close to the common gulls, I must in fairness mention that I never once saw any of their race search for or carry away an egg or young bird.

On leaving the Outer Hebrides, my way led me to the upper reaches of the Spey. Here is at least one large colony of the common gull, and in conversation a certain well-known sportsman gave it as his opinion that the damage worked by this gull was slight. I think I was able to convince him that the contrary was the case, in Uist at all events, although the habits of gulls vary in different districts. There is no doubt that, in the central Highlands, the common gulls steal many ptarmigan eggs, and I have seen broken eggshells lying thickly in the shallow waters of a hill loch on which the gulls nest.

The young common gulls grow fast, and as early as July 10th — just a month after the time of their hatching — the first was seen on the wing during the summer of which I write. From being most anxious and excited over their downy young the gulls gradually came to regard a boat landing at their island with indifference, and after mid-July the island was deserted by them.

Meanwhile, on the adjoining island, the black-headed gulls had been having a wretched time of it. A colony of rats were established on the island, and as fast as the unhappy gulls laid their eggs the rats devoured them. This went on until the very end of June, when the gulls left the island gradually, without having hatched a single chick.

I could not help thinking it would have been more appropriate had these rats established themselves on the common gulls' island!

In appearance the common gull is not unlike the kittiwake, but is a trifle larger, and on the wing is not quite so graceful — its wings seeming more blunted.* But in their habits the two birds are entirely different, for the kittiwake prefers the open sea and wild headlands, whereas the common gull is more at home on land than at sea. Compared with the black-headed gull the common species is somewhat heavier in build and less buoyant in flight.

In winter, when the tribe of the common gull are spread out over the British Islands, they may be seen often following the plough, doubtless acting as the farmer's friend by devouring harmful grubs, such as the larva of the 'daddy longlegs' fly. So that this good must in fairness be set off against their unfortunate habits of the summer.

---

* *The wings of the kittiwake are black-tipped; those of the common gull are black to near the extremity, which is white.*

CHAPTER XXVI
The Short-Eared Owl

THERE ARE few birds abroad upon the moorlands of the Outer Hebrides. Grouse are scarce; no curlew or golden plover cheer the summer dawn with their wild whistling notes. The moors are dreary and very silent in May and June. But there is one bird found upon the South Uist moorlands which is met with seldom on the Scottish mainland — and that is the short-eared owl.

As you wander through long and old heather, with a cold clammy fog driving in from the Atlantic in grey banks, you see, perhaps, rising a yard or two ahead of you, a curious silent-flying bird. It makes its way — a buff-coloured object — with very slow wing beats over the moor. One would think that its apparently feeble wing-thrusts would fail to carry it against those storms that so frequently sweep the Hebrides, yet upon these gale-swept islands it finds a congenial home.

It was during the last days of May that I came across the first nest of the short-eared owl. Upon a boggy glen the sun shone warm. It was one of those rare days when the sky was blue, and the Atlantic had momentarily lost its sullen appearance. As a friend and I walked up the glen the early morning mists were still low. Many crofters were at work cutting their peats; into the still air rose the smoke of a small peat fire, where later they would brew the tea for their midday meal.

As we reached the top of the little glen the sky showed blue in patches. Hitherto all the hills had been hidden, but suddenly, and with fine effect, the top of Beinn Mhor appeared above the mist, the sun striking full upon its rocky and storm-scarred summit.

Then, one after another, the lesser hills appeared, and the fog lifted from off the sea, so that the long breakers curling beyond the green machair gleamed white in the sunshine, and the innumerable lochs that bordered the shore reflected the deep blue of the sky.

From some heather a short-eared owl rose at our feet. The nest was there — a slight depression scraped in the heather. In it there crouched a brood of three white down-clad owlets. The eldest was a full fortnight old; the youngest had seen the light but a few days. All owls are peculiar in that they lay their eggs at intervals, and do not wait, as do most other birds, until the last egg is laid before commencing to brood. The young of the owls are also interesting in that they have two complete coats of down during their early weeks.

Backward and forward above us the old owl flew, calling anxiously and angrily.

Her barking cries soon attracted her mate, who, on his arrival, threw himself into the heather nearby, feigning injury in order to lead us from his brood, and calling with a curious note, difficult to reproduce. It was interesting to see that the parent owls seemed little or nowise inconvenienced by the intense sunlight and strong glare. At such close quarters one occasionally could note them blinking with human-like movement of the eyes. And how many people, I wonder, know that the owls differ from other birds in that the upper lid, as in ourselves, closes the eye, instead of the lower? But the tribe of the owls are unlike us human beings in that they have a well-developed 'third eyelid', or nictitating membrane which may be used to shade the eye in strong light and also, perhaps, to clean it — whereas in ourselves this third eyelid is but rudimentary.

So intense was the anxiety and so repeated the cries of the parent owls that a third short-eared owl made its appearance. It came from farther up the glen, and showed only a mild interest in ourselves, though it evidently sympathised with the emotions of the two harassed parents.

As we left the home of the short-eared owls banks of white fog were creeping shoreward from the Atlantic. From the rocks an old man was laboriously cutting fucus, or bladder seaweed. This, in a creel, he very slowly carried to his little field. Near him another couple were working in their croft. Although the morrow would be the first day of June, the oat crop had not been sowed as yet. As we watched, the seed was scattered by hand. Manure, scattered by hand also, was then strewn upon the field, and ultimately the crop was harrowed in, by hand likewise.

Just two weeks later I visited the nest of the short-eared owls. The peat-cutters had been busy in the glen, and had been working near the nest. The owls had evidently moved their brood — they were too young by far to fly of their own accord — and although the nest was deserted, the parent birds fluttered about me with excited cries. A careful search failed to reveal the owlets, and I did not see them again.

But in the soft light of a Hebridean evening, an hour or so before midnight, I more than once marked the short-eared owl fly silently across the rough, stone-scarred moorland with its innumerable lochs. One night, when the almost incessant wind had dropped for a while, and when soft clouds covered the sky, the short-eared owl passed and settled unafraid upon a boulder near me, a dignified bird, with an air of profound wisdom about it.

The short-eared owl is more migratory than most of the owl tribe, and is better known in many parts of Scotland as a passing migrant in spring or autumn, than as a nesting species. From its migratory habit it is in some places known as the 'woodcock owl'. Outside the British Islands it has an extremely wide range. It is found throughout the greater part of the European and North Asiatic continents, North Africa, and North and South America. It nests, too, beyond the Arctic

Circle, and as far south as the Mediterranean. In the British Isles it is most common as a nesting species in the Orkneys and Shetlands and in the Outer Hebrides.

The short-eared owl preys on mice, rats and voles, and is of inestimable benefit to the agricultural community. During vole plagues the birds lay much larger clutches of eggs than under normal conditions, and as many as fourteen eggs have been found in a nest!

It is harmless to game, and should never be destroyed, although keepers too often class owl, hawk and grey crow together as vermin. Yet this destruction is absolutely indefensible in the case of the short-eared owl. About thirty years ago a great plague of field voles descended upon Selkirkshire, 15,000 voles being killed in one small district in a month by men armed with wooden spades. Towards the end of the plague no fewer than 400 pairs of short-eared owls were living in the district, and so great was their vitality from their abundant diet of field mice they reared two large broods in the course of the summer.

As showing the destructiveness of owls towards mice, the late Lord Lilford found that a half-grown barn owl swallowed in quick succession no fewer than eight of these small animals. The ninth it swallowed – all but the tail! The same authority calculated that a pair of owls, catering for their brood, accounted for perhaps a 150 mice and rats in the course of a single summer's night – for they visit their young with food almost continuously. Thus it can be seen that each pair of owls shot means a very large increase in the numbers of mice and rats in the district.

CHAPTER XXVII
The Hen Harrier

NOW A rare bird everywhere in Scotland — it has been banished entirely from the mainland of that country — the hen harrier lives out its furtive life upon mist-swept islands of the Hebrides and the Orkney and Shetland group.

And yet at one time it was common, not alone in Scotland, but in England as well. Its very name shows that it was then a formidable menace to the poultry yard, and its nest was as often as not built in the fields, within sight of prosperous farms.

But man's hand has been heavy against the hen harrier, for wherever there has been game preserving it has been mercilessly shot, although its food is chiefly — like that of the short-eared owl — young rabbits, mice and rats. Is it not known to Gaelic-speaking Islesmen as 'the mouse-hawk'? And it is curious to see how owl-like is the harrier, in its habits as well as its food. It has the same soft, ghostly flight, the same unobtrusive ways. It does not, like the eagle, sail proudly high in the azure fields of the sky, nor, like the peregrine, stoop earthward at lightning speed after its prey. It beats methodically and leisurely across the moor, now and again dropping silently to the heather to pick up some over-bold field vole, or even some hurrying beetle it has spied.

So greatly do the male and female hen harriers differ in plumage that for long it was surmised they were of two distinct species. The male bird is one of the most handsome things that flies. His upper parts are of a pale slate-grey; the tips of his wings are black; the rump and the hinder parts are white. Pie is about two inches shorter than the hen. Beside him the female is a drab and inconspicuous bird, dark brown on the upper parts, but resembling the male in that she has a white rump. Across her tail are five dark bars.

In his handsome plumage the cock harrier is visible afar as he flits without haste across the silent moorlands. He calls seldom, for he hunts by stealth, not by boldness. Perhaps the most remarkable thing about him is his habit of crossing the same strip of moor at exactly the same hour each day. He is so punctual one can almost set one's watch by the time of his passing.

I doubt whether it has ever been realised what extensive areas of moorland the harrier traverses in his hunting, for, although his flight is slow, it is effortless. I have many times watched him — I say 'him' advisedly, for the hen from her inconspicuous colouring is difficult to locate — and have noted the extreme precision of his line of flight, and also the great distances he travels. When hunting the harrier always moves against the breeze, and I have watched him fly downwind at express speed to that part of the moor where he was in the habit of commencing his foraging. Turning and facing the breeze he proceeded leisurely to search the hillside. Each little hollow was carefully scanned, and following as he did the contour of the hill so closely, the harrier frequently disappeared from view for a few seconds, and thus was difficult to keep under observation. Once he settled on the moor and stood awhile as though resting. His speed was perhaps 20mph, and I should say that this is the average rate at which a harrier moves when hunting.

On the evening in question the bird captured nothing so long as he was in sight, though he momentarily paused more than once as though his keen eye had glimpsed a fleeting mouse. It was after ten o'clock at night – the season was midsummer – when this particular bird of my acquaintance was in the habit of taking his last flight, but, of course, he hunted through the day as well. One morning when on each hill tarn the sun shone brightly, and when the moorland was warmed so that the scent of the heather was a very pleasant thing to experience, the cock harrier was spied hunting up wind, as was his custom. His course was above a hill burn, and for long, now hovering kestrel-like, now moving forward on silent wing, he scanned the ground below him. At length he dropped to the ground, and rose with a mouse's nest in his talons. Apparently the mouse was elsewhere at the moment, and the harrier passed out of view without having found game.

For some time before the nesting season the harriers soar buzzard-like above the moorlands as they search for a suitable nesting ground. One day of early May I watched a female harrier sail across a large loch. She alighted on a boulder on a hill above me, and called several times. Then, from the blue sky the male appeared. Settling near her, he stood awhile, then, since she still called, from time to time bowing as she did so, he flew across to her, and mating took place. A few days later I again saw the harriers crossing the hill, one of the pair frequently rising almost vertically into the air and then 'stooping' in play to within a few feet of the ground. Towards the end of May, in a corrie, with a deep, peaty loch and precipitous rocky slopes on three sides, three harriers were soaring.

As they played, they called with a whistling high-pitched cry, not unlike the note of the buzzard. The third bird was apparently unattached – her mate may possibly have been out of sight – and in the end the paired birds flew off into the mist, the cock swooping down upon a grey crow that had aroused his dislike. The harriers' nesting ground is usually long heather, and the same little glen or hillside is sometimes resorted to year after year. But if a pair of grey crows should take up their home in the glen (they are the earlier nesters of the two, and thus have built their nest some weeks before the harriers have thought of family affairs) the hen harriers will seek out a new nesting site.

The nest is composed of heather. For that of a ground-nesting bird, it is a large structure, yet the length of the heather on which it is built renders it invisible except at close quarters. The harrier, even when its nesting ground is disturbed, is a silent bird. A keeper, on whose ground a pair usually nests, tells me he is generally able to locate the nesting ground from the curious behaviour of the cock bird. As he flies over the spot where his mate is brooding, the male dips to the surface of the heather, clapping his wings together and uttering a high-pitched note.

Even in its remaining strongholds the hen harrier has become so scarce there must be considerable inbreeding, and my own experience seems to show that some of the pairs are barren. It seems to be only a question of time before this handsome bird shares the fate of the kite and the white-tailed eagle, for even to its most inaccessible nesting grounds collectors make their way each year, and to a collector a clutch of hen harrier's eggs is a prize of the first order.

Since it is a shy bird, the harrier nests in the most out-of-the-way moors and glens. I shall always remember a long tramp across sunlit moors, beneath a sky of the most exquisite blue, to a remote haunt of the hen harrier. The air was still and very' hot. In a little corrie, filled with long heather, the harriers had their nest. As I approached the hen arrived, apparently bringing food to the family. The cock, who had been on guard at the nest, thereupon took wing, and flew off to his hunting. I had already seen him, an hour or so previously, searching a hillside nearby.

As I approached the nest the hen took wing, and one, if not two, of the brood accompanied her with hesitating flight. Beside the nest when I arrived there remained one full-grown youngster, its brown plumage harmonizing so closely with the dark heather that it was scarcely visible. A few yards from the nest, what was apparently the nest of the previous season just showed among the heather. Curiously enough, during the time I was at the nest the parent bird never once put in an appearance, though she cannot have failed to observe my approach. The young of the hen harrier, when fully fledged, are in plumage a dark brown colour. They thus — whichever their sex may be — resemble their mother during the first year of their life, for the young males do not assume the handsome pale slate-grey plumage until they are fully mature.

At the nesting ground were numerous castings. These castings are the indigestible remnants of the harrier's food, and are ejected from the bill in the form of pellets. It was interesting to find in the pellets the wing cases of many beetles, showing that the hen harrier, like the kestrel, feeds largely upon these insects.

Besides hunting the moorlands, the harriers regularly visit the sand dunes, where they prey on young rabbits during the summer months. No more charming picture can be imagined than a still summer evening, soft sunlight and an atmosphere of peace brooding over land and sea, with the harrier sailing upon Vshaped wings in the light of the westering sun as the bird crosses with effortless flight the close-cropped grassy land that fringes the shores of the Islands of the west.

Although in Scotland the hen harrier is on the verge of extinction, outside of the British Isles it has a wide distribution. It is found throughout Europe, south to Northern Spain, Central Italy, and South Russia. In Lapland it nests up to 69 degrees north latitude; it also breeds in East and West Siberia.

In winter it ranges south to the Sahara, and it is probable that some of the young birds reared upon the Scottish islands migrate southward. Certainly scarce a season passes without one or two being reported from the mainland, both of Scotland and North England. They usually meet an untimely fate, for every keeper is ready to bring down so tempting and unsuspecting a target.

CHAPTER XXVIII
The Decrease of Game Birds in the West

IT IS now generally admitted that game birds — especially grouse and black game have very largely decreased along the Atlantic seaboard during recent years. The probable causes of this decrease, and the problem of whether these West Highland moors can be restocked, are matters of great importance to many.

Up to the middle of last century most of the shooting was done by the landowner, and perhaps the poacher, too, for his own pot. Then the monetary value of a grouse moor from the sporting point of view gradually rose as facilities of access to the Highlands increased, and owners commenced to let their ground to shooting tenants. A 'close time' was enforced by law, but as the tenant often took the moor for one season only, no doubt he endeavoured — and naturally — to account for as many red and black grouse as possible. Since stocks commenced to diminish, a limit was placed by the owners on the number of birds to be shot in the season.

Old books and records show that the enemies of game birds a century or two ago were fully as numerous as during recent years, and were considerably more varied. Eagles abounded; kites and hen harriers (now almost extinct) were everywhere. Ravens, too, were far more widely distributed than at the present day. Yet, in spite of the great abundance of all these varieties of so-called 'vermin', grouse and game birds of all kinds were plentiful.

The problem we are confronted with at the present time is to find the cause of the present scarcity of game on the West Highland and Island moors.

It seems to me that there are several reasons for this lamentable decrease in grouse; no single factor is sufficient to account for it. The most probable causes appear to me to be: firstly, changes in the climatic conditions of the Atlantic coast, which have caused the birds to migrate east; secondly, the gradual decrease of the heather areas and consequent increase of grass and bracken; and thirdly, the indiscriminate shooting of grouse in former days (before close time and limits were instituted), which unnaturally depleted the stocks of breeding birds. In the west, grouse moors and sheep farms are often on the same ground, and while the sportsman wishes to conserve the heather, the farmer is anxious to burn as much of it as possible. There is thus a conflict of interest, and an unsystematic burning of the moor. The popular belief is that the decrease is due to the multiplication of the natural enemies of game birds, which took place while the owners and keepers were absent during the Great War.

What are the natural enemies of grouse? The golden eagle amongst the Cairngorms in Central Scotland is numerous, yet never were grouse and ptarmigan so plentiful as during last autumn (1922). There is little doubt that the hoodie crow and the greater black-backed gull are the game bird's worst feathered enemies. Other gulls, such as the lesser black-back and common gull, are harmful to a lesser degree. But I am convinced that some other reasons must be sought for the remarkable decrease in grouse and black game during the past seven years.

Let us take the case of a certain Hebridean island. Here the grey crow is not common, the buzzard is unknown, there are no eagles or sparrow hawks, gulls are less numerous than formerly, yet grouse, thirty years ago plentiful, are now almost extinct. On this island the hills are infested with rats, and to these rodents the scarcity of grouse may be partly due.

The hoodie crow is a formidable enemy to the grouse. There is no bird so fond of eggs as he is. One pair alone may account for over one hundred grouse eggs in a month, for their instinct for locating the nests is remarkable. Often a pair work together, and when a sitting grouse is found, one hoodie will entice the hen bird off the nest, while the other villain steals up behind and sucks the eggs! Hoodies are not above swallowing grouse chicks also.* As destructive as the hoodie, though in a different way, is the greater black-backed gull; yet, fortunately, he is nowhere numerous. This large and powerful bird devours the young rather than the eggs of the grouse, but not content with this, chases the old grouse themselves. When flying in the normal way the wing-beats of the great black back are slow and almost laboured; but when in pursuit of a luckless grouse his flight is quick and purposeful, and the grouse is almost always overtaken. Its one chance of escape is to plunge into long heather, where it is more or less safe from its fierce enemy. The great black back and the hoodie should be ruthlessly shot, and their nests harried whenever possible.

The lesser black back, the herring gull and the common gull all take both eggs and young of the grouse, and are not to be encouraged, though their predatory habits vary much in different districts. It should be remembered, too, that these species of gulls, together with the black-headed gull, are the farmer's friends, in that they eat the 'leather jacket' and other harmful grubs.

With regard to birds of prey, the golden eagle does more harm by scaring the birds than by the numbers it actually kills. It does not find the capture of grouse an easy matter, and prefers to take hares and rabbits for the feeding of its young. The same thing is true of the buzzard, and I doubt if anyone has actually seen a grouse struck down by that bird, or found a grouse carcass in a buzzard's eyrie.

---

* In June, 1923, I found no fewer than 40 sucked grouse eggs on a small island near where hoodies were nesting.

The peregrine falcon is an enemy of grouse, but it is nowhere so numerous as the buzzard. I have seen a peregrine nesting on a well-stocked grouse moor, with nesting grouse within a hundred yards of the eyrie and quite unperturbed by the presence of the hawks. But this may have been due to the fact that the peregrine, like the eagle, does most of its hunting away from home, in order, no doubt, not to betray its nesting site.

The sparrow hawk is a bad bird on a moor, but the kestrel is often unjustly blamed, and it is most beneficial in keeping down the mice and beetles, which form its entire food. The merlin — a fine, dashing little hawk — is nowhere sufficiently numerous to do much harm. The common rook and the carrion crow are inveterate egg stealers.

Fox, weasel, stoat and rat are all enemies of game birds, but they cannot be held responsible for the decrease of grouse in the Western Islands. In Mull the fox is now extinct, and in the Outer Isles there are no foxes, weasels or stoats, though here, as I have mentioned, the rats do much harm.

That grouse have decreased to an alarming extent is shown by the following figures from two western moors: 1914 — 112½ brace. 1915 — 96½ brace; a big stock left on the moor. 1916 — 79½ brace. 1917 — only 10½ brace! 1918 — 7 brace. 1919 — 18 brace; moor let that season, and shot very hard. 1920 — 4 brace only. Thirty miles were covered to account for these eight grouse!

The figures from the other moor are: 1916 — 112½ brace (although there was only a small stock of birds on the ground at the end of 1915). 1917 — only sixteen brace; an extraordinary drop. 1918 — 7½ brace. In the course of his letter the owner of the latter moor states: 'In 1916 I could easily have shot 250 brace on a limited area of 1500 acres. On the other 8000 acres scarcely any grouse were present. In mid-October, 1916, during exceedingly wild and wet weather, the whole stock vanished with the exception of a few odd scattered birds. Not a bone or feather left behind. I have no doubt in my own mind they simply migrated in a pack, never to return. I am equally sure the parent birds were a migrating pack of the previous season. They probably did not arrive much before the nesting, or they would have been more distributed. The good old 'vermin' theory is, I contend, enormously exaggerated. I often used to hear an old keeper give it as his opinion that when the heather in Lorne did not ripen the grouse cleared off in packs, all going east, mostly by Glen Orchy, though never south.'

It will be seen from the above figures that on these two moors — and they are typical of many — grouse have now almost ceased to exist, and at the same time the bags obtained on the central and eastern moors of Scotland have been steadily on the increase during the last few years. As regards the west, the most interesting point is that there was no gradual decrease — the falling off in numbers was sudden and extreme. During the summer of 1916 a heavy stock of grouse was on the moors. In October of that year the weather was exceptionally stormy, and there were very heavy rains, even for the west coast over 4½ inches of rain in twelve hours at Fort William — so it seems probable that these great storms caused a wholesale migration of grouse from the Western Highlands.

In 1915 over a score of blackcock assembled each spring morning on the shores of a Hebridean sea loch. Now there is not one. They vanished during the stormy winter of 1915-16. That red grouse do migrate is proved by the account of a reliable correspondent. He tells me that one day last winter from 400 to 500 grouse passed over Balquhidder, flying steadily north-east, about twenty feet from the ground.

What steps are to be taken to re-establish on the western moors their former stock of birds? It seems to me that a judicious and careful burning of the heather is fully as important as an attempt to exterminate the natural enemies of the grouse. But more important than anything is fine and moderately dry weather, for so long as the present mild and wet winters persist, grouse will never thrive and become abundant in the Western Isles. By all means keep down the hoodies and the gulls, but let it not be forgotten that there is a 'balance of nature' which works in a very mysterious, and often little understood, manner, and which easily can be upset by man's interference. The famous scientist Charles Darwin proved that the presence of many owls and kestrels in a given area caused an abundance of clover. For this useful fodder plant must be fertilised by bumble-bees; these make their nests in the ground, but are destroyed by field mice. When, however, the field mice are kept down by owls and kestrels, the bumble bees, and hence the clover, thrive exceedingly. In such an intricate and delicate manner does Nature preserve the right balance of living things, and it is often to man's own disadvantage to interfere. The sudden spread of grouse disease will, perhaps, one day be proved to have been due to some upsetting on man's part of the delicately adjusted balance of Nature.

Let there be more time given by keepers and owners to the study of what food the birds of their moors do live and prey on; let the cases against them be proved conclusively before they are ruthlessly exterminated, and the risk incurred of some greater evil than we yet know of sweeping away all our game birds. Once our hawks and eagles are exterminated, they will not come back again, and even should no disease or other pest take their place, much of the romance and poetry of the wild life of the Highlands will surely be gone forever.

INDEX

INDEX

127

INDEX